art_ists in schools

a
handbook
for
teachers
and
artists

Caroline Sharp

Karen Dust

The revised edition of the Handbook was sponsored by:

National Foundation for Educational Research
Calouste Gulbenkian Foundation
Paul Hamlyn Foundation.

About the authors

Caroline Sharp is a Senior Research Officer at the NFER. She has considerable experience of research studies in all sectors of education and was Project Leader for the Artists-in-Schools research. She has written numerous reports and books on arts education, including: a report on the arts in primary teachers' initial training; several publications on instrumental music services; and a survey of discretionary awards for students in dance and drama.

Karen Dust works part time as Education Officer at Eastern Arts, one of the English Regional Arts Boards. She is a director of a small, independent film and video company and also freelances as an arts and education consultant, researcher and writer. Recent work has included editing special needs publications for UNESCO and working with the National Lottery Department at the Arts Council of England.

Photocopying

Published in March 1997
by the National Foundation for Educational Research,
The Mere, Upton Park, Slough, Berkshire SL1 2DQ

Cover Design by METAPHOR
Book Design by Tim Wright

Contents

Acknowledgements

We would like to express our gratitude to the original sponsors of the research as well as to the sponsors for this edition of the Handbook. The original sponsors were:

National Foundation for Educational Research

Arts Council of Great Britain

School Curriculum Development Committee

Calouste Gulbenkian Foundation

and

British Petroleum Company PLC.

The sponsors who enabled us to produce this new edition of the Handbook were:

National Foundation for Educational Research

Calouste Gulbenkian Foundation

Paul Hamlyn Foundation.

We are grateful to the people who took the time to read and comment on the draft of the Handbook:

Gordana Bjelic-Rados, artist

Judy Bradley, Assistant Director, NFER

Patrick Redsell, Performing Arts Adviser, Suffolk Education Department

David Sheppard, Manager, Norfolk Arts in Education Service

Michele Tallack, Director of Artists in Schools Diploma, Anglia Polytechnic Universty

Pat Trickett, Head of Music, Tile Hill Wood School.

We are also grateful to Tony Knight, Professional Officer at the School Curriculum and Assessment Authority for his comments on part of the text.

We would like to thank all the artists, teachers, pupils and others who contributed to the original research; the RAB and National Arts Council officers who provided information for the revised edition; and the NFER staff who prepared the book for publication, in particular:

Effie De Souza, secretarial work

David Upton, technical editing

Enver Carim, overview of publication.

Introduction

This handbook is for teachers who want to work with artists and for artists who want to work in schools. We have written it for primary and secondary teachers and teachers of children with special educational needs, regardless of their level of arts expertise; and for artists who are interested in working in schools, whatever their experience of this type of work. The term 'artist', which is used throughout the book, includes arts professionals working in the performing arts, literature, visual arts, crafts, media and multimedia.

The guidance offered here is drawn from the findings of a two-year research study of the work of artists in primary, secondary and special schools located throughout England and Wales. The research was based on case studies of projects in 25 schools, including observation of work in progress and interviews with about 200 pupils and over 70 of the artists, teachers, heads and others involved. The case studies were backed up by a survey of all the English Regional Arts Associations (now Regional Arts Boards) and interviews with about 30 individuals who had extensive experience of artists-in-schools work.

This is the second edition of this book. Since the first edition was published in 1990, both education and the arts funding system have gone through a period of major restructuring which has affected the nature and content of artists-in-schools work. Despite funding constraints, there is a continuing interest in partnerships between artists and schools. A number of training programmes have been set up for artists wishing to work in schools, and there has been a developing understanding of the factors underpinning successful projects. In 1996, this area of work received a new impetus, with the announcement from the Arts Council of England that artists-in-schools projects were to become eligible for funding from the National Lottery, under the *Arts for Everyone* programme.

This new edition of *Artists in Schools* is funded by the NFER, the Calouste Gulbenkian Foundation and the Paul Hamlyn Foundation. It has been extensively rewritten and updated. In aiming to provide practical information, we have added more sample documents and photocopiable materials to help guide artists and teachers through the process. To ensure that the advice on current opportunities is as up to date as possible, we carried out another survey of the English Regional Arts Boards and contacted the National Arts Councils for England, Wales, Scotland and Northern Ireland, the British Film Institute and the Crafts Council to find out about their current policies and roles in artists-in-schools provision. We have examined current practice in this area and taken account of documents which have been published since we first wrote the book.

Finding your way around

We begin with an overview of the potential of artists-in-schools work: exploring the benefits to pupils, teachers, schools and artists; describing the approaches artists can take to working in schools; and discussing some of the frustrations that can occur. This is followed by detailed guidance on each stage of a project for both artists and teachers. There is advice on getting started, planning and the project in action. There is also a chapter devoted to evaluation strategies. The book ends with an extensive resources section, which provides a listing of contact organisations and relevant publications. We hope you find the book useful in planning, running and evaluating your project.

benefits and frustrations of artists-in-schools work

In this chapter we use the research findings to:

- discuss the main benefits of artists-in-schools projects

- outline three types of involvement for artists

- illustrate some of the things that can go wrong

- describe the features of successful projects.

The chapter ends with a description of the features of successful projects and a summary of the main points.

Benefits of artists-in-schools work

This section outlines the potential benefits of artists-in-schools projects for pupils, teachers and schools, and artists. Naturally there are areas of overlap, since something that benefits pupils is also of value to teachers, schools and to artists themselves.

Benefits for pupils

Artists-in-schools projects can contribute at many levels to pupil learning in, through and about the arts. They can also provide role models for pupils and opportunities for them to develop positive relationships with adults other than their teachers.

An insight into the professional arts world

The professional arts can seem very separate from the everyday experiences of children and young people. It is quite common for pupils to admit that they have never thought about professional artists before one visits their school, or that they have only ever heard about the work of great artists of the past. Young people interviewed in the research often commented on the different perspective that meeting a 'real live artist' had given them.

Pupils are fascinated to hear about where artists work, how they publicise their work, how long it takes to write a book, make an artefact or create a performance. They can find out how artists feel about presenting their work to the public (and to critics) in exhibitions, publications and performances, and about the technical, commercial and business skills involved. The commitment and dedication of artists show pupils that working in the arts is a serious business. As one pupil said: 'I never realised there was so much to it.'

Pupils who are given the opportunity to find out about these areas of an artist's life begin to see artists within the context of 'the world of work'. Artists can talk about how and why they became an artist, the training they have undertaken, and some of the routes into their profession. For some pupils, especially those who are beginning to think seriously about possible careers, talking to artists can give them insights into what might be involved in working in the arts. Contact with artists also gives teachers the opportunity to discuss the contribution of the arts industries to the economy.

Understanding artistic processes

Working with professional artists helps pupils to recognise that there is a process behind finished pieces of art. As one pupil commented: 'All we used to do before was just see the finished thing; we didn't know what happened in the making of it.'

Pupils can learn how artists gain inspiration from a variety of sources, including: their own experiences and environment; their own and other cultures; historical and contemporary sources; and the work of other artists, past and present. Pupils can find out about the importance of research in helping artists to develop their own work or to interpret the work of others. They see how artists rework their ideas many times, experimenting with different ideas and progressing from one piece of work to the next.

Some artists help pupils to learn about the origins and traditions of their art forms. For example, one of the pupils who worked with a dancer commented: 'I liked it because he explained things to us. Instead of just showing us the dance, he told us about the traditions of the dance and when it started.'

Trying new approaches

Many pupils who work alongside professional artists demonstrate their willingness to try out an artist's approach for themselves. For example, one secondary school involved some of its students in a writing residency. The students described how their teachers had often encouraged them to redraft their work, but they had seen this as a chore, and redrafting had become little more than a process of copying out their original piece of work in neater handwriting. Working with a writer, however, had impressed on them that 'writing is not as easy as you think. You can't just put anything together and think it's finished.' Many of the pupils commented on the process of redrafting that the writer himself went through: 'He changed one line, then changed it again and again until he got it right.' Pupils who had previously found writing 'boring' became motivated to redraft their work several times. As one girl who took part in the residency commented: 'It can't be right the first time. I read my work and think: no, this can't be right; this needs to go here and that needs to go there.'

Developing artistic skills

Some of the artists-in-schools projects we studied enabled pupils to learn skills in an art form new to them, such as creative dance, photography, opera, crafts or puppetry. Other projects aimed to help pupils to develop and extend existing skills in areas such as drama, creative writing, music-making and painting.

As pupils begin to apply their new skills, they also acquire knowledge and learn new concepts. To take one example, secondary students involved in a weaving residency watched a craftsman demonstrate some basic techniques (how to begin to weave; how to use a bobbin; and what to do when they wanted to introduce a new piece of yarn). They practised these techniques for themselves and then worked on a piece based on their own designs. As they put their new skills into practice, they made many discoveries about the nature of weaving, including that a woven image is built up by putting the background in place first to 'support' the main image. They discovered that designing for weaving requires a different approach from making working sketches for a painting. As a result of this new understanding, they began to simplify their original designs and to concentrate on introducing colour and texture into their work.

Artists can help young people to develop skills in presenting the arts. Many projects provide opportunities for pupils to share their work with each other, with their teachers and with parents. In this situation, pupils discover how to put together displays and performances which will appeal to a defined audience.

Working with professional artists can help children to develop and apply skills of critical appreciation. For example, the education officer of a major opera company described how a group of six-year-olds had worked with some of the company members on making their own opera. The pupils then visited the company to see a performance of *A Midsummer Night's Dream*. Their comments afterwards showed that they had a good understanding of the creative processes involved in staging the opera, and had learned the language needed to discuss the performance in some detail.

Enthusiasm, enjoyment and confidence-building

Pupils often comment on artists' enthusiasm for their work. For example, pupils involved in a music-theatre project commented that company members were 'all enthusiastic, and they helped us to be the same'. It is valuable for pupils to see adults displaying an uninhibited and open enthusiasm for arts activity. Older students who have reached the age when there is strong peer pressure to appear disinterested, can be won over by an artist's commitment and enthusiasm.

Raising the status of the arts in the eyes of pupils helps those individuals who want to be involved but lack the confidence to stand up to negative comments from their peers. Sometimes an artist's presence in a school can be a catalyst for pupils being more open about their own interest in the arts. In one example, a secondary student explained how disappointed she had been when she was put in the lowest 'set' for English at school. She admitted that she often wrote poems at home, but hid them in a drawer and never showed them to anyone else. When her school had a writer's residency, she was keen to take up the opportunity. She later commented that sharing her work with a professional writer had greatly improved her confidence in her ability to write.

Pupils learn from the artists' own approach: 'If they don't mind being fools and singing out loud,' said one girl, 'then you think to yourself, why am I so shy?' Many pupils find that artists encourage experimentation, and that this helps to build up their confidence. One pupil commented: 'If you had an idea and you thought it **might** work, he'd say go ahead with it, whereas before you'd think: if it's not going to work, it's a waste of time.'

Role models

Artists can be important role models for pupils. For example, some pupils identified strongly with artists who were black, disabled, or who presented positive examples of successful men and women (one pupil admitted that meeting a female painter had been a surprise: she had automatically assumed that 'the artist' visiting her school would be a man).

If pupils meet someone in a professional role within the school with whom they can identify as being 'like me', it can help build their self-confidence. As an Afro-Caribbean dancer explained: 'The black children can identify with me: it can give them positive images of black people and inspire confidence in themselves.' Similarly, a disabled dancer demonstrated that it is possible for someone using a wheelchair to achieve in an art form which many people assume is the preserve of the able-bodied. His example encouraged disabled children to participate with confidence and enthusiasm.

Positive working relationships

The relationships built up with individual artists or company members often have a lasting influence on the pupils concerned. Young people relish the opportunity to work with adults who show respect for them as 'fellow artists' and take a personal interest in their work. Pupils from different projects spoke of artists being 'really interested in our work', and 'treating you more like a **person** than a pupil'. One girl commented: 'I expected some toffee-nosed, stuck up, well-dressed bloke. But when I got there, he was more my level, not higher than me — more like a best friend.'

Benefits for teachers and schools

Involving professional artists (especially in longer-term residencies) can help schools to broaden their coverage of the curriculum, develop the skills of the teaching staff, and make links with the wider community. Working alongside artists can have both professional and personal benefits for teachers. Artists have much to offer schools, especially in the new, more competitive educational climate.

Artists-in-schools projects which give consideration to the needs of teachers (e.g. through a specific in-service element) can help teachers in a number of ways, including: introducing what the project will involve, helping them to gain insights into the artist's way of working, and developing their artistic skills.

Contributing to the arts curriculum in primary schools

All schools now teach English and drama, art, music and dance as part of the National Curriculum. This can be challenging for primary schools, as they may not have specific arts expertise among their staff. Many teachers of younger pupils have had limited opportunities for training to teach arts subjects, and some therefore understandably lack confidence in teaching the arts.

In one case teachers from a junior school wanted to use clay more often with their classes, so they invited two ceramics workers to visit the school. Before the project began, a group of teachers took part in a two-day course led by the ceramics workers. The teachers said that they had learned several new techniques, and gained the confidence to use clay with their classes. One teacher commented: 'I always thought I was no good at art, but this changed my mind.'

Contributing to the arts curriculum in secondary and further education

In addition to work at key stage 3 (i.e. for 11- to 14-year-olds) secondary schools can find it helpful to work with artists to develop the curriculum in relation to specific courses of study for older students, such as the General Certificate of Secondary Education (GCSE), General National Vocational Qualifications (GNVQs) or A-level studies. The same is true for further education and sixth-form colleges, although they are more likely to employ artists as part-time lecturers.

Many secondary school arts teachers are themselves practising artists at an amateur or semi-professional level. For these teachers, working alongside an artist provides opportunities to discuss the arts at a professional level. In addition, artists-in-schools projects can benefit arts teachers by raising the profile and enhancing the status of the arts in the school.

Contributing to the arts curriculum for pupils with special educational needs

Children with special educational needs (SEN) have 'an entitlement' to the National Curriculum, which means that their teachers are working to the same basic curriculum framework as teachers of other children. However, as is sometimes the case in primary schools, many teachers of children with special needs have had limited arts training opportunities and therefore lack experience and confidence in teaching the arts. Working with a professional artist can open doors for these teachers and provide the impetus and ideas for the development of the arts in their own teaching.

Artists can provide a fresh stimulus for all pupils, but this is a particularly important benefit for children with special educational needs. Many of the teachers who took part in the research found that it was difficult to provide fresh stimuli within a special school or unit's daily routine. The opportunity to work with an adult who is not a teacher is in itself a stimulus, but an artist offers a particular opportunity, working in a way that requires an aesthetic and emotional response from the pupils. This can motivate learning in other areas; for example, in language work. One teacher interviewed during the research commented that an artist's visit had 'widened' her pupils' language. She had talked with them about their physical and emotional experience of music-making and dance, and together they had found ways of voicing their response to the work.

The arts can facilitate the growth of aural, visual, linguistic, motor and social skills and these are all important aspects of learning for children with special educational needs. However, because there is so much that these children can learn through the arts, the aesthetic side of their arts experience can be overlooked. But the children's learning **in** the arts is just as important as the learning they do **through** the arts. This is particularly so for those whose learning difficulties or disabilities do not disadvantage them in arts activities, as they then have a chance to excel. A positive experience of this kind can increase a child's self-image and sense of self-worth.

There is an important difference between involving children with SEN in arts activities and 'arts therapy'. Arts therapy involves using an arts activity as a method for diagnosis and therapeutic intervention. Arts therapy should be undertaken by a trained therapist, but involving children with SEN in arts activities is part of their educational entitlement.

Observing another adult working with their class

For teachers working in all sectors, having another adult enter their domain and work with their class is a challenge which offers opportunities for reflection on their own approaches to teaching.

Many teachers find that they benefit from seeing an artist working with their classes. As well as learning new artistic techniques and observing the artist's approaches to working with young people, some teachers find it particularly valuable to see how individual pupils respond to another adult who has different expectations of them.

Developing teachers' interest in the arts

Teachers sometimes find that working with artists has a major effect on their own attitudes towards the arts. For example, a primary teacher nearing retirement was thrown in at the deep end when his class was assigned to a dance project at the last minute. He was initially 'appalled' to find the project 'dumped' on him, but by the end of the project he felt differently. 'I found a new vision of dance,' he said. 'Once I had committed myself, I thoroughly enjoyed it. I can't wait to do dance with my new class.'

Enriching the whole curriculum

Professional artists provide an educational resource, helping a school to enrich and develop its curriculum. Artists are perhaps most commonly thought of as contributing to the arts curriculum, but many artists use their skills to contribute to other subjects too. We learned of artists working in virtually every area of the curriculum, including: exploring scientific concepts through theatre-in-education; drama and written work inspired by historical events; and visual artists and musicians working with information technology.

Dealing with personal and social issues

The arts engage people at both an intellectual and an emotional level: they provide a useful medium for schools to help pupils to encounter, discuss, and understand complex and difficult areas of human experience.

Some artists and companies choose to address issues of equal opportunity, such as race, gender or disability. Some help schools work on other sensitive issues, such as health and interpersonal relationships (e.g. addiction, sexual health, bullying).

In one case, a theatre-in-education company was invited to perform in a primary school. The play presented positive images of black and disabled people, and dealt with themes of disability and racism, which the teachers later developed with their classes. In another example, a painter's residency provided opportunities for GCSE students to discuss issues of cultural identity and to develop this theme through their choice of subject matter and style for their own paintings.

Developing closer relationships with pupils and other staff

In some schools, teachers taking part in the research found artists-in-schools projects had helped them to form closer relationships with other members of staff and with pupils.

In one case, the staff of a secondary school wanted to work more closely together. A group of ten teachers planned an integrated arts project which involved staff from different subject areas working with small groups of Year 8 students. When interviewed afterwards, teachers said that they felt the project had helped to improve morale and that they had built up good working relationships with the staff and students who took part. One teacher said: 'I have never seen the staff take to anything in such a single-minded and cooperative way, considering that these people represented such a wide range across the school.' Another commented: 'The teacher-child barrier got broken down by the small groups working together and with purpose.'

Some projects give teachers and pupils a chance to work with others from different age-groups and abilities. For example, an arts week was held in a school which had a special unit for pupils with moderate learning difficulties. The project included pupils from the unit working in integrated groups with the mainstream pupils. Many of the mainstream pupils said that they had been surprised by the capabilities of the pupils from the unit, and felt that these children had made a positive contribution to the group work. This project was highly successful in breaking down barriers between teachers and pupils from different parts of the school.

Making links with other schools

Several of the artists-in-schools projects studied in the research involved groups of schools working together, in some cases for the first time. Examples included: links between mainstream and special schools; between schools teaching similar age-groups; and between neighbouring schools serving different age-groups (e.g. nursery–infant–junior or primary and secondary schools).

Teachers who took part in projects involving other schools felt that both they and their pupils gained a great deal from cooperating with others, building new relationships and sharing ideas and resources. There were examples of these links persisting after the projects had ended, with teachers continuing to meet to plan new initiatives in the arts and other areas of the curriculum.

Involving parents and the wider community

Artists-in-schools projects can be a good means of attracting the interest and participation of parents. Parents are an important part of both the school and the local community. They can be involved with a project in a variety of ways (e.g. through fundraising, participation in workshops, and attendance at project events). Teachers who inform and interest parents in artists-in-schools projects find that this contributes to the pupils' enthusiasm for the work.

As well as working with pupils and teachers, an artist's residency can provide opportunities for the involvement of the wider community. Many schools have an active policy of such involvement and see themselves as a community resource. Use of school facilities by a variety of groups is growing, and some schools regularly involve the local community in their activities.

An artist can run open sessions for the public or for specific community groups (e.g. people attending an adult learning centre, an amateur arts group, or a senior citizens' club). If the artist is working on a commission which will be seen by members of the public, local people can be consulted and involved in the commissioning process.

Even if the community is not involved directly with the artist, displays, exhibitions, screenings or performances of work associated with an artists-in-schools project can be held in public venues, such as galleries, libraries and local arts venues.

Promoting a positive image of the school

Schools often find that artists-in-schools projects are of potential interest to journalists: such projects provide good opportunities for photographs and features in the local press. Similarly, photographs of young people working alongside professional artists, and of the resulting performances and displays, can look good in the school prospectus.

In some cases, projects include a commission from the artist for a piece of work. This is most likely to be a visual arts or crafts piece, such as a sculpture, mosaic, painting, or wall hanging, which is designed for a particular location in the school. However, schools may commission writers, composers and film-makers to produce a new piece of work for or about their school. Such commissioned pieces can enhance the school's environment, add to its artistic resources, and/or provide a cultural and historical record of the school, its pupils and staff.

Benefits for artists

As far as artists are concerned, one of the obvious benefits of working in schools is financial: educational projects provide opportunities for artists to supplement their often limited incomes. For some artists, such as members of theatre- or dance-in-education companies, working in schools is the main focus of their artistic activity. For others, such as writers, visual artists and craftspeople, artists-in-schools projects enable them to gain access to school facilities and equipment which they can use in producing their own work. Some schools are willing to offer artists free studio space in return for the artist spending time working with pupils and teachers. So, although no money changes hands, both sides gain from the arrangement.

However, money and access to facilities are not the primary motivation for most artists. The majority choose to work with young people because they get a great deal of enjoyment and satisfaction from it. Those working in areas of personal and social education usually do so from a sense of commitment to the benefits of this kind of work.

Reaching a wider audience

The motivation for an artist to work in schools often springs from a desire to reach as wide and diverse an audience as possible. Some artists are frustrated with the 'exclusive' label of the arts, and relish the challenge of making their art form accessible to people who would not normally choose to engage with it. As an Indian dancer said: 'I wanted to perform something that would be meaningful in the present day. I used to do some dance classes in the Indian classical style, but all the children who came were Indian.' She explained that by working in schools she aimed to make Indian dance 'accessible to all ages, races and backgrounds'.

Working with others

For artists who work alone for much of the time, artists-in-schools projects provide opportunities to meet and interact with others. Several artists commented on the 'seclusion' of both their training and much of their working lives. For visual artists, craftspeople, writers and composers in particular, artists in-schools projects provide opportunities to improve their communication skills and to learn from the way in which adults and children react to their work. As one painter explained:'I usually only discuss my work-in-progress with other artists, and they tend to comment on the technical aspects of a painting. I find it good to discuss my work as I do it; I find I learn a lot from people's comments and reactions.' A composer made a similar comment: 'Seeing the way students react, and the ideas they have, makes me see things I've excluded from my work. It makes me think again.'

On the whole, the influence of pupils and teachers on the work of artists is indirect rather than direct, although one writer involved in the research was inspired to write a series of poems about the young people he encountered during his residency in a school.

Helping others to develop their abilities

For many professional artists, the rewards of working in schools come with the pleasure of helping staff and pupils to develop their skills and to become motivated to participate in the arts. Some artists have the satisfaction of knowing that they have provided the stimulus for young people's interest in the arts, which will help to build the artists and arts audiences of the future.

Artists typically describe working in schools as 'intensive, exciting and exhausting'. Many artists would not want to work in education full time, but find that artists-in-schools projects are an interesting, challenging and important part of their working lives.

Three types of involvement

There are three main types of involvement for artists working in schools. Artists can take the role of maker, presenter or instructor/facilitator. Each type of involvement contributes to pupil learning, but does so in a different way.

Making

Making emphasises the process of professional art-making from initial ideas to 'finished' performance or piece of art-work. The artist concentrates on making his or her own piece of work on school premises (sometimes as a commission for the school).

- Projects which show the artist as maker enable pupils to observe a particular creative process.

- A commissioned piece of work contributes to the school environment and serves as a long-term reminder of the artist's visit.

Examples: visual arts, crafts and writing residencies.

Presenting

Artists **present** a completed piece of work to an audience in a school.

- Presentation enables artists to bring high-quality arts experiences into schools.

- It demonstrates the performance skills of professional artists (e.g. actors, story-tellers, dancers and musicians).

Examples: writers giving readings from their work; musicians giving concerts and recitals; theatre- and dance-in-education performances; live art performances and events.

Instructing/facilitating

When artists take on the role of **instructor/facilitator,** they help pupils and teachers to make and/or present their own work (e.g. by demonstrating techniques and working alongside pupils and teachers).

- Artists help pupils and teachers to be practically involved in the arts and to become makers and presenters themselves.

- Because the artist has enabled teachers and pupils to develop their skills, there is potential for related work to continue in the school after the project has ended.

Examples: could be any art form; workshops and residencies.

Combining approaches

Each of the three types of involvement is valuable in its own right, but the greatest benefits are to be found when artists-in-schools projects combine two or three approaches.

Adopting just one type of involvement has potential disadvantages: for example, an artist who is solely involved in making his or her own work, without the direct involvement of pupils and teachers, is in danger of being treated as a 'live exhibit' on show to the rest of the school. Presentation is valuable, but if pupils and teachers do not have a clear understanding of the context of the work and an opportunity to explore the issues raised, they can be left wondering how to respond. Artists who are confined to the role of instructing/facilitating (e.g. simply demonstrating artistic techniques) can be mistaken for teachers by the pupils, who then miss out on the special experience of working with a professional artist.

By combining approaches, schools can maximise the benefits of arranging for a professional artist to visit the school. Most projects use two or three approaches, although they may emphasise one of them. Instructing/facilitating is the most common element, and this is valuable because it provides the most direct contact and interaction between artist and pupil, and enables pupils and teachers to build up skills which they can transfer to new situations after the artist's visit has ended. Here are two examples which show how artists can successfully use more than one type of approach.

Case study: making and instructing/facilitating

An artist was commissioned to make a sculpture for a sixth-form centre. He began his residency by discussing ideas with staff and students. He put up posters inviting students to meet him and to offer suggestions for inclusion in the sculpture design. He also invited students to visit a local exhibition of his work. Although the main emphasis of this residency was on making a sculpture for the centre, students were able to participate by contributing to the artist's design process, and by learning more about his work. A small group of students also worked with the sculptor, making their own pieces of work.

Case study: presenting and instructing/facilitating

A children's writer visited a rural primary school for the day. The pupils had prepared for the visit by reading several of the writer's books, and by deciding on the questions they wanted to ask her. The writer spent the morning talking to a group of 30 pupils about her work. She explained that many of her books and short stories were based on incidents from her own childhood. She read one of her short stories to them which explored the theme of 'fear'. She then asked the pupils to tell her about times when they had felt afraid. The session ended with an opportunity for the pupils to ask their questions.

In the afternoon the writer held a workshop with 12 pupils from the morning's group. She introduced a writing task and provided some stimulus material. When she was sure that the pupils understood the purpose of the exercise and how to approach it, she asked them to write for 20 minutes. At the end of the session, the children read out what they had written and the writer commented on each piece of work.

The head said: 'The two stages of the day were necessary, i.e. the writer talking about herself, her books and her ways of writing and then transferring that to working with the children on their writing.'

There are many other examples of artists successfully using more than one of the three approaches. Performers, such as members of theatre, dance and opera companies, often combine a presentation of their work to a large audience with workshop activities for smaller groups of pupils. Some companies and individual artists work alongside pupils, demonstrating the process of art-making and putting together a joint display or performance for the school, parents and the wider community.

A particularly good way of emphasising the professional artist's role as maker and/or presenter is to arrange two-way visits. The artist or company visits the school and the pupils and teachers visit the artist or company. A visit to an artist's studio, a gallery or a theatre, when combined with work in a school, shows pupils the professional artist's working environment and helps them to understand who artists are and what they do.

What could go wrong?

Although all of the projects we studied had some benefits for pupils, teachers and artists, few were seen as an unqualified success for all concerned. Some frustrations arose which could often be traced back to the way in which projects were originally initiated and planned.

This section uses descriptions from some of the artists-in-schools projects studied in the research to illustrate common problem areas. It offers suggestions for avoiding problems and/or dealing with them when they arise.

Lack of support for artists

Several artists reported examples of projects in which they had felt poorly supported in schools. In some cases, they were used as 'supply teachers', helping to plug a gap in a school's arts provision. In other cases, artists were placed in schools with recognisably poor provision in the hope that their presence would 'convert' teachers to a new way of working. This kind of situation, not surprisingly, could lead to resentment from the staff members

concerned and to isolation for the artists, who were put under pressure by having to 'carry' the project alone. Although there were occasional success stories in these cases, on the whole they created poor artist–teacher relations and consequently affected the impact of the work in the school, as demonstrated in the following example.

Case study

An artist was invited to work in a secondary school, with two art teachers and their classes. Although one of the teachers was strongly committed to the project, the other had become involved at a later stage and was not particularly interested in what the artist had to offer. She agreed to take part, but explained that she was not willing to have her curriculum 'disrupted' by the artist's presence. Things began badly and rapidly got worse. One day the teacher left the artist alone with the pupils for most of the time. This led to a chaotic session, with the artist struggling to maintain order among a class of 12- and 13-year-olds. In subsequent sessions, the teacher stayed in the room, but retreated to a far corner to do her marking. Although some of the pupils in this class made positive comments about the project, the artist admitted to feeling 'angry and frustrated over this situation being allowed to develop'.

Sadly, this was not the only example of its kind. Several artists spoke of teachers who 'made their excuses and left'.

Advice

● Projects which do not have the active support of the teachers involved have a poor chance of success. Artists should be wary of taking on work involving staff who do not show a commitment to the project.

benefits and frustrations of artists-in-schools work

- There is a better prognosis for a successful outcome if there is a core of interested and enthusiastic teachers, and the project has support from someone in senior management (e.g. the head of department or headteacher).

- Artists should never be left in sole charge of a class.

Unprofessional behaviour from artists

There were some reports from teachers of poor practice from artists. Teachers were angry with artists who cancelled at short notice, did not turn up on time, were poorly prepared or expected teachers to do all the work.

Advice

- When selecting an artist for a project, schools should look for evidence of the artist's understanding of the constraints of working in schools.

- Teachers should take up artists' references, checking for evidence of a professional approach in their previous work.

- Artists should clarify with schools exactly what is expected of them. Once committed to a project, they should honour their agreement to carry out the work.

- Schools should make it clear to artists exactly what will be expected of them. This should be agreed and detailed in writing (i.e. in a contract).

Confusion about what the project is aiming to achieve

It was fairly common for the teachers and artists involved in the research to admit that they did not fully understand the purpose of a project. Sometimes artists and teachers had firmly held but very different ideas about what a project was attempting to achieve. Artists and teachers were angry when their initial expectations were not fulfilled and relationships could become strained as a result.

Case study

A secondary school was offered the chance of a two-week residency with two artists. The teachers and company members met to discuss the purpose of the residency and agreed that the artists would make a large mosaic based on designs prepared by students. The teacher coordinating the project expected the artists to involve students in designing and making the mosaic.

In the event, although they used elements from the students' designs, the artists worked on the design for the mosaic in private. They then concentrated on making the mosaic themselves. In general, the students were not involved in the process, and the artists did not interact with them. The teacher was pleased with the final mosaic, but was disappointed with the lack of student involvement. One of the students commented: 'I got really switched off; I thought **we** were going to do it. I thought the whole point was for us to see **our** designs translated from a piece of paper into a mosaic.'

In this case, teachers and artists had not fully discussed the purpose of the residency before it took place, neither had they really understood each other. This resulted in students and teachers feeling disappointed and let down.

Advice

- Teachers and artists should check that they have a common understanding of the purpose of the project and the way in which this will be achieved in practice.

- It is important to have a clearly expressed set of aims and objectives for the project.

- Before the project begins, time needs to be set aside for joint discussion between artists and teachers to allow them to reach a common understanding and plan to realise each of the project's aims.

Teachers' resentment of the artist's role

One of the problems that occasionally arises during a residency is that teachers feel envious of the artist's position. Artists can be seen as privileged people, able to come into a school and work intensively with one group of pupils without having to deal with the day-to-day routine of teaching. Teachers who are practising artists themselves may feel that having a 'real' artist visit the school undermines their professional status as artists in their own right. Also, if an artist has different methods of working with pupils, or gives advice that runs counter to that of teachers, unexpected resentment can result (e.g. if an artist encourages free experimentation, while the teacher is concerned to ensure that students produce an acceptable piece of work for their GCSE folders).

Advice

This is a difficult area to deal with, not least because it is not always easy for people to admit that there is a problem.

- Artists need to be sensitive in their approach to working in schools and to avoid undermining the teacher's status or methods of teaching the arts.

- Artists and teachers should find out how their approaches differ from each other, and discuss the implications for the project.

- If problems of this kind do occur, it is important for both sides to recognise what is happening and to discuss how to put things right (it could be useful to seek advice from a third party, such as a project coordinator, or LEA adviser).

A lack of pupil commitment

Some pupils involved in artists-in-schools work admitted that the purpose of the project had never become clear to them. Talking to these pupils, we discovered that they had never really 'connected' with the project or understood why the artist had come to work in the school.

A few of the teachers interviewed in the research chose not to tell the pupils about a project in advance. This stemmed from a concern that pupils would become over-excited or worried about their involvement with artists, or from a desire for the project to arrive as 'a nice surprise'.

However, interviews with pupils demonstrated the need to inform them about the work and their role in it. As one group of pupils explained: 'Our teacher didn't really know what we were doing, and it turned out to be nothing like we expected.' One girl added: 'I didn't like not knowing. I think they should have told us what they were going to do.' Projects which gained a high degree of commitment from pupils were those where the pupils knew and understood the aims of the project from the start.

Advice

- Pupils need to be informed of the purpose of the artists-in-schools project and what will be expected of them.

- Pupils need information about the artist who will be working with them.

- The process of monitoring and evaluation should include pupils' views.

Involving too many pupils

There are understandable pressures on schools to ensure that as many pupils as possible come into contact with a visiting artist. Because of this, artists are sometimes heavily timetabled, working with too many pupils. Artists find it exhausting and disheartening when they are unable to work with any one group in sufficient depth, or when groups are too large. Such projects can only have a limited impact on the pupils concerned.

Advice

- Rather than spreading the artist's time thinly with a large number of pupils, projects should focus on a smaller group of pupils, with opportunities for other pupils to have more limited contact with the artist, if desired.

- Teachers could consider changing the timetable to enable an artist or company to work with one group of pupils for a sustained period of time.

- Artists can stipulate a maximum number of pupils with whom they wish to be involved, and a maximum number with whom they are willing to work in any one session.

Too much pressure

Some artists-in-schools projects attract a great deal of attention from both within and outside the school. Teachers, artists and pupils involved in the research sometimes felt that they were under too much pressure to talk to visitors, to present work and, above all, to demonstrate that the work was providing value for money.

There was often pressure for pupils to produce a finished 'product' to show to parents and the rest of the school. Of course, such pressure can have positive results — many pupils commented on how they had learned to put something together quickly, to work as a team and to be aware of the needs of the audience. If the project has been designed to include a performance, sharing or exhibition as a major outcome, then this pressure can become an important part of the learning process. In some cases, however, artists and teachers regretted having to 'force the pace', because it reduced the time available for exploration and experimental work.

Advice

- Artists and teachers should try to be realistic in their expectations of what can be achieved in a given time.

- Visits of people not directly involved (e.g. those wishing to see the work in progress) should be managed so that they do not distract from the work itself.

- There should be a detailed timetable, which is used to monitor progress during the project. Artists and teachers should be prepared to adapt their initial plans during the project in order to achieve a successful outcome.

Lack of evaluation and feedback

Some artists feel frustrated because they do not hear about the impact and development of their work after they have left the school. Many would welcome some positive criticism of their work to help them improve and develop. Similarly, teachers often find that there is no time to reflect on projects, before the pressure begins to move on to something new. An evaluation report is often required by sponsors: sometimes evaluation is seen as an additional burden on teachers and artists, at a time when all available energy is being devoted to the project itself.

Advice

- Artists and teachers should try to view evaluation as a positive opportunity for participants to reflect on and develop their practice.

- Artists and teachers should build in manageable strategies for monitoring and evaluation.

- A feedback meeting should be a planned part of the project.

A way forward

This chapter has outlined some of the main benefits of artists-in-schools projects. The fact that we have devoted much more space to the potential benefits than to the things that could go wrong reflects our evaluation of the positive contribution of this kind of work. The following chapters provide guidance to help artists and teachers minimise the problems and plan for a good working relationship with benefits for artists, teachers, schools and, most importantly, for young people.

Features of successful projects

From the findings of our research and our reading of the reports of other projects and schemes, we have identified the following features that characterise successful projects.

- The project addresses a school need.

- The project builds on the strengths of artists (e.g. artistic/technical knowledge and skills) and teachers (e.g. teaching skills, knowledge of the curriculum and of their pupils' needs). Artists are not expected to be substitute teachers.

- The project is part of the ongoing work in the school: the school provides a context, support for, and development of, the artist's contribution.

- Artists and teachers are committed to making the project a success. There is a real sense of partnership between artists and teachers, which is built up through negotiation of the project's aims and content.

- The project's aims are ambitious yet achievable. There is a shared understanding of the aims and how these are to be realised in practice.

- The budget supports joint planning, review and evaluation as well as funding contact time between artists and pupils.

- The project is targeted at a specific group of pupils, but there are opportunities to share the project with others in the school (teachers, pupils, parents and governors).

- Pupils are briefed about the project. They are given an opportunity to experience the artist's work and to learn about the professional context in which the artist operates, as well as a chance to participate in practical activities.

- There is a project evaluation which contributes to a review of practice and to forward planning for both artist and teachers.

Summary: benefits and frustrations of artists-in-schools work

Through working with professional artists, pupils can:

- gain an insight into the professional arts world
- learn about the process of art-making
- transfer some of the artists' approaches and methods to their own art-making
- develop their existing skills and learn new techniques
- benefit from positive role models
- experiment, take risks and become more confident in expressing themselves
- experience a different approach to learning
- develop a positive relationship with a fellow artist.

Through working with professional artists, schools can:
- enrich the arts curriculum
- contribute to teachers' professional development
- help teachers to introduce a new area or course of study
- benefit pupils with special educational needs
- use the arts as a medium for learning about other subjects
- focus on sensitive personal and social issues
- develop closer relationships between pupils and staff
- make links with other schools
- involve parents and the wider community
- promote a positive image of the school.

Through working in schools, artists can:
- find a source of employment and gain access to resources
- reach a wider audience
- derive a sense of achievement from helping young people confront difficult issues
- break down the isolation of working on their own
- discuss work in progress and observe audience reactions to their work
- experience the pleasure of helping staff and pupils to develop their artistic skills and interests
- help to develop the next generation of artists and audiences.

There are three main approaches that artists take to working in schools:
- making
- presenting
- instructing/facilitating.

Some of the things that can go wrong during artists-in-schools projects are:
- a lack of support in schools for artists
- unprofessional behaviour from artists
- confusion about what the project is aiming to achieve
- teachers' resentment of the artist's role
- a lack of pupil commitment
- involving too many pupils
- too much pressure
- a lack of opportunity for feedback and evaluation.

an artist's guide to getting started ②

This chapter is for artists who are interested in working in schools and would like some guidance on getting started. It should also be relevant for artists who already have some experience but want to explore new areas of work.

The chapter starts with a questionnaire designed to help artists who are new to this kind of work. The rest of the chapter contains guidance on:

- the education system

- gaining relevant experience and training

- building good relationships with pupils

- safety issues

- what to charge

- how to find work

- preparing information for schools

- negotiating projects with schools, including questions to ask at interview

- taking a booking.

An artist's questionnaire

The following questionnaire is designed for artists who are considering working in schools. The questionnaire may be photocopied. Once you have completed the questionnaire, you may find it helpful to talk through your answers with a friend or colleague. Ideally this should be someone with experience in this area who can offer some advice on how to follow up your ideas.

The objectives of this exercise are to:

- give you an idea of what might be involved in schools' work

- help you to decide whether you want to pursue this type of work

- identify what you have to offer to schools

- clarify what kind of involvement would suit you best

- provide a basis for your next steps towards working in education.

Activity

Think about yourself, your background and skills. Then answer the following questions as fully as possible, noting down the reasons for your answers in the space for comments.

A. You and your work

1.
a) Why do you want to work in schools? (Tick all that apply.)

To reach a new audience	◯
To reach a young audience	◯
To make your work more accessible	◯
To work with young people	◯
To get a first-hand reaction to your work	◯
To help others to develop their interest/skills in the arts	◯
To work in other areas (e.g. science, technology, history)	◯
To work with young people on personal and social issues (e.g. racism, sex education)	◯
To gain access to school facilities and equipment	◯
For financial reasons	◯

For other reasons (please add)

b) Look at the items you have ticked: which of these are most important to you?

Comments:

2. What skills and qualities do you have to offer schools? (Tick all that apply.)

Professional knowledge and skills

Knowledge of the commercial/professional arts world

Background knowledge about your art-form (or chosen issue)

Specific art-form skills

A particular way of working which starts from the artist's perspective

An ability to produce high-quality work

Other skills (please add)

Personal skills and qualities

Good communication skills

Enthusiasm for your art-form

Patience

Reliability

Good organisational skills

Ability to work under pressure

Motivation to make things work

Other qualities (please add)

3. In Chapter 1 (pages 8 –11) we highlight three types of involvement for artists working in schools. Which of these approaches would you feel most comfortable with?

Making ⬭

Presenting ⬭

Facilitating ⬭

Comments:

4. Which elements of your work do you think would be particularly interesting to young people?

Comments:

5. Which elements of your work could be adapted for/are already suitable for work with young people?

Comments:

6. a) How do you feel about working with young people?

Comments:

b) Which age range(s) of young people would you most like to work with?

under 5s ☐   5 - 11 ☐   11-13 ☐   14-16 ☐   16-19 ☐

Comments:

7. Would you consider working with children who have special educational needs?
(See page 27.)

Comments:

B. Your suitability for working in schools

8. Do you enjoy talking to people about yourself and your work?

Comments:

9. How do you feel about the thought of people watching you at work?

Comments:

10. Would you enjoy working alongside other adults (e.g. teachers and parents)?

Comments:

C. Practical issues

11. What length of involvement would you be able to commit to, given your work patterns and ongoing commitments? For example:

half or one-day visits

projects which involve blocks of time in school (e.g. three days at a time)

projects which require a regular commitment over a period of time (e.g. one day a week for two months).

Comments:

12. How far are you willing to travel to work in schools? (How would you get there?)

13. What safety issues might be involved? (See page 29.)

Feedback

Having got this far, ask yourself the following questions, or better still discuss them with someone else.

- Do I still want to pursue this area of work?

- If so, what type of work do I want to focus on?

- Is there anything I need to find out more about before I try to find work?

- Do I need any experience and/or training before I would feel confident about approaching schools?

What you need to know about education

If you have not worked in schools before, it will help you to know:

- what types of school there are
- what they teach (the curriculum)
- how they are organised and run.

You do not need a comprehensive knowledge of the education system to work in schools, but there are some things it would be useful to understand. The following information is relevant to the education system in England and Wales. Readers who live in other parts of the UK and those who already have an understanding of the education system may wish to turn straight to page 28, which deals with getting relevant experience and training.

Local education authorities

Local education authorities (LEAs) offer a policy lead on the curriculum and other areas of development, and most run in-service training (INSET) for teachers. Although the government's funding for schools is mainly channelled through LEAs, they retain very little for central functions (such as running artists-in-schools schemes). However, most LEAs have specialist advisers for at least some arts curriculum areas.

Local management of schools (LMS)

All LEA schools receive an annual budget allocation from the LEA and are responsible for managing their own budgets. The amount they receive is calculated using a formula, based on the number and ages of pupils in the school. The formula is different in each LEA. Once a school has received its annual budget allocation, it is free to spend the money as it wishes. The money is not earmarked for specific purposes.

Grant-maintained schools

A school can 'opt out' of LEA control if a parents' ballot has been held and the majority of parents have voted in favour of the school leaving the LEA. The school then becomes 'grant-maintained': it receives its funding direct from central government, generally via the Funding Agency for Schools.

Independent schools

Independent schools are funded by parental fees. They do not have to abide by the National Curriculum, although many choose to do so.

School governors

Most governing bodies are made up of parents, teachers, local business people and, in the case of LEA schools, representatives of the LEA. The governors control the school's budget and make all major funding decisions (on advice from the headteacher).

The National Curriculum

English schools are required to provide for the spiritual, moral, social and cultural development of their pupils. Schools must teach the National Curriculum, which comprises ten foundation subjects, of which three are called 'core' subjects.

- English ⎤
- Mathematics ⎬ core subjects
- Science ⎦
- Technology (design and technology and information technology)
- History
- Geography
- Modern foreign languages
- Art
- Music
- Physical education

Drama is taught within English, and Dance within PE. (The curriculum is very similar in Welsh schools, with the addition of Welsh language teaching.)

Key stages

The education of children aged five to 16 is divided up into four key stages.

Key stage	Pupil ages	School years
1	5 – 7	1 and 2
2	7 – 11	3, 4, 5 and 6
3	11 – 14	7, 8 and 9
4	14 – 16	10 and 11

Not all subjects are required to be taught at all key stages: pupils do not learn a modern language until they are in Year 7, and the arts are optional after the age of 14 (the end of Year 9).

In Years 10 and 11, most pupils follow GCSE (General Certificate of Secondary Education) courses. Some pupils begin GNVQ (General National Vocational Qualification) courses in Year 10.

If you want to know more about the National Curriculum — what it contains and how it is structured and taught — we suggest you get hold of some of the publications listed on pages 105–6.

Special educational needs

Children with special educational needs (SEN) are those for whom special educational provision is necessary. Approximately two per cent of children are educated in units attached to ordinary (mainstream) schools or in special schools. However, it is expected that the needs of the majority of children with SEN will be met in mainstream schools. Mainstream schools usually have a person responsible for coordinating provision for special educational needs, often referred to as a SENCO (special educational needs coordinator). Children with SEN are entitled to access to the same educational opportunities as other children, including the National Curriculum.

The main areas of SEN are: emotional and behavioural difficulties; mild, moderate or severe learning difficulties; specific learning difficulties (dyslexia); visual or hearing disabilities, other physical disabilities and exceptional ability.

If you want to find out more about this area of work, contact the LEA Adviser for Special Educational Needs. See also national arts associations and networks (page 98) and books on special educational needs (page 107).

Getting relevant experience and training

It will be easier to find work in schools if you have some relevant experience and/or training. To get some experience, you could start by making contact with teachers in a local school. Try suggesting a visit to some relevant lessons to observe or to help with activities. Once you have built up a relationship with a teacher, he or she may be willing to talk through your ideas, suggest some contacts, and act as a personal referee when you are seeking work in other schools.

There are training courses for artists wishing to work in education, and many of the English RABs offer bursaries to artists attending them. The availability of training courses depends on the area in which you live, although some RABs may be prepared to offer bursaries for artists attending courses outside their area. The National Arts Councils may also be able to provide training opportunities and/or bursaries.

Some RABs run short courses themselves, or fund other agencies and arts organisations to run them. Typical examples include courses on workshop skills and on working with students with special educational needs. Some RABs hold surgeries and seminars for artists working or wishing to work in education. At the time of writing, there are two long artists-in-schools courses available in England.

- To get some relevant experience make contact with teachers in local schools.

- Find out about training opportunities in your area by contacting your RAB (if you live in England) or National Arts Council (elsewhere in the UK).

See Resources, pages 97–9, for contact details of the RABs and National Arts Councils.

Building good relationships with pupils

You need to consider how to build good relationships with pupils. Pupils involved in residencies sometimes form strong personal relationships with artists and company members. These relationships stem from mutual respect and understanding. Occasionally pupils tell an artist things that are private to them: you are advised to respect pupils' confidentiality in these circumstances.

Case study

The quotations given below are taken from pupils' comments about artists who had different approaches to working with young people. The first comment is from a Year 10 student involved in a poetry residency.

'If you take your poem to a teacher, they say "That's wrong"; and I think: "That's mine; you can't tell me it's wrong". But when I took a poem to [the poet] he just changed two words around, he didn't take anything away… he just changed it round to make it flow better, and I liked that because he asked me.'

In contrast, here are two Year 5 pupils talking about a visual arts residency:

'I didn't like drawing the figures on paper, but the drawing was good, and then [the artist] came over and spoilt the picture by making the wriggerly lines thicker.'

'I particularly enjoyed it when we were painting, but I didn't like it when she spoilt my picture when we were doing green, and she came and did light green. And she moaned at us because we used brown.'

These examples illustrate the fact that pupils like artists to discuss changes and suggest improvements, but do not like artists to alter their work. The approach taken by the writer in the first example generates respect: it helps pupils feel that their opinion matters and that they too can be 'artists' in their own right.

Making sure your work is safe

Teachers will want to be reassured that you are a suitable person to have access to their pupils. You must make sure that your working practices are safe, especially where pupils are concerned. Your own safety, and that of your property, are other issues that need to be considered.

Protection from child abuse

Everyone who works in education has become acutely aware of their duty to protect children from possible harm from visitors to a school, and it is in your interests not to be placed in a situation where an accusation of abuse could arise.

- A school is likely to ask you for references, and may require a criminal background check to ensure that you do not have any convictions for a sex offence.

- It is wise to avoid situations where you are in one-to-one contact with an individual young person for a sustained period of time, particularly in an isolated part of the school.

Ensuring safety

You need to think carefully about everything you are planning to do in a school and identify any potential hazards. This includes considering the needs of children with allergies and other health problems. For example, a theatre group used make-up on children's faces without checking that it was hypo-allergenic. Unfortunately, one child came out in a rash, much to the annoyance of his parents and teacher.

Issues of safety are most likely to arise if you are

working with groups of young people, for example during physical activities. Safety is also an issue if the school is planning for a group of pupils to visit your workplace.

- Make sure that your working practices are safe, and take extra precautions where potential hazards are concerned (e.g. use of sharp tools, chemicals and kilns).

- Discuss the proposed work in detail with teachers, pointing out any potential dangers and the steps you will take to avoid accidents.

- Ask for a teacher to be present whenever possible, during work with pupils.

- If teachers are planning to bring a group of pupils to visit you, make sure there are no obvious hazards in your workplace. It makes sense to discuss relevant safety issues with teachers in advance of their visit.

See also page 104 for publications on safety issues in schools.

Insurance

If you are self-employed, it is your responsibility to arrange and pay for appropriate public liability insurance (which will provide cover for any legal action arising from accidents to pupils and staff occurring during a project). It is possible that the school's insurance may cover this, even if you are self-employed. If you are to be considered an employee of the school for tax purposes, then it is the school's responsibility to arrange for appropriate insurance.

Self-employed artists should take out appropriate personal insurance against injury and illness during a project. You should also make sure that your property is safeguarded and insured while in the school. This is particularly important if you are taking expensive equipment or valuable pieces of art into the school.

● Most artists' organisations can advise on appropriate insurance cover for artists working in schools.

What to charge

You need to decide what you are going to charge schools.

● There are recommended minimum daily/ sessional rates for artists working in schools. Contact the relevant artists' organisation, National Arts Council or English Regional Arts Board for details of the 'going rate'.

● You should charge for contributing to in-service training for teachers and attending project meetings, as well as for contact time with pupils.

Finding work

Before you begin to publicise your availability for artists-in-schools work, it will help to have clear, thought-through answers to the questions in the artists' questionnaire (pages 19 – 25). You can find work in several ways, including: answering advertisements in artists' magazines (such as *Artists Newsletter*); using local information networks; putting an entry on to a database; and by direct mailing to schools.

Networks

Although your potential employers will generally be schools, you may find work in schools through umbrella organisations which run artists-in-schools projects. For example, there are agencies which

market artists-in-schools schemes directly to schools and arrange work for artists registered with them.

It is a good idea to contact your RAB (in England) or National Arts Council (elsewhere in the UK) to find out how artists-in-schools work is organised in your region. Ask to speak to the relevant art-form officer (or education officer, if there is one). These people can advise you about who to contact locally and will have names and addresses for the people and organisations listed below.

The main contacts are:

● National Arts Councils and English Regional Arts Boards

● arts and arts education agencies

● arts organisations

● local authority arts officers

● local education authority (LEA) advisers and advisory teachers

● individual artists who have some experience of artists-in-schools work.

See pages 97–100 for a listing of the main contact organisations.

Databases

RABs and National Arts Councils either have their own databases of regional artists available for work in schools or can direct you to an agency which holds a database. Some of these are in a printed format and some are computerised. There are also a few slide directories which contain photographs of artists' work.

● Artists wishing to be included on a database should contact their RAB or National Arts Council.

Direct mailing

If you wish to contact schools direct, begin by targeting those within a certain radius of where you live. Your chosen radius may cover more than one local education authority, which will mean that you have to make contact with key people from two or more LEAs. You will find a list of local schools in your telephone directory or at the library. You could telephone your LEA and ask for a list of schools, although some authorities charge for providing this information.

When contacting schools, send publicity material to a named teacher if possible (you can find out the name of the teacher responsible for the appropriate area of work by ringing the school secretary). You may decide to follow up a publicity mailing with a telephone call, but wait at least two weeks before doing so. Teachers receive mountains of paper and even if they do wish to follow up an idea, they will usually have to obtain permission from the headteacher first, which will take time.

Producing publicity material

Your publicity material will probably be the first contact a teacher or agency will have with you, so it should reflect something of your professional arts activity and your preferred approach to working in schools. Its content and presentation should motivate whoever is reading it to contact you to find out more.

Content

Schools will want to know about:

- your training and experience as an artist

- any training and experience you have had working with young people in schools or other settings

- the art form(s) in which you work and what you do

- what you can offer to schools, including your skills, ways of working and relevance to the curriculum

- where you are based and how far you are willing to travel

- the ages of pupils you are willing to work with

- whether you are interested in work with pupils with special educational needs

- what you charge and whether this is negotiable for longer projects

- referees — preferably previous employers who have experience of your work in schools, but otherwise someone who is familiar with you and your work.

Design

Whether you design the material yourself or work with a professional designer, it will help to consider the following questions.

- What job do I want this to do (e.g. introduce you as an artist, explain what you are offering to schools, sell the idea of having an artist in the school, sell the idea of a commission) ?

- How long will the person receiving the information have to read it?

- How can I make the information visually interesting?

- What style of presentation will best reflect my work and what I have to offer?

- What can I afford (e.g. how many colours on a leaflet, size of leaflet, number to have printed)?

- Will the material be cheap and easy to mail (e.g. will it fit into a standard sized envelope and how heavy will it be)?

Information and resource packs

Some companies and artists who work in schools prepare packs of information about themselves and their work. This is not simply publicity material: the purpose of an information pack is to give teachers more information about you and how you work so they can prepare for your visit. Artists do not normally send a pack to a school until there is a firm commitment to the project.

There are two main types of pack: general information packs and project-related packs. You need to decide what type of pack, if any, is appropriate to each project. If you do decide to put a pack together, you may find it useful to seek advice from someone with relevant teaching experience who could offer help with content and presentation. Some suggestions as to what you might include in each type of pack are given below.

General information pack

This is most suitable for short-term involvements. The pack could include:

- a biography and c.v. giving information about your training and professional arts activity (e.g. exhibitions, productions, performances)

- reviews of your work

- photographs of your work and/or you at work

- detailed information about your work, the artistic processes involved and how you might adapt these in the classroom. For example, if you are a dancer, do you specialise in a particular style? What approach do you take to choreographic work?

- details of your usual requirements when working in a school, such as materials, space, facilities (e.g. access to running water)

- some suggestions for linking your work to the National Curriculum and/or examination syllabuses.

A project-related pack

It would be worth designing a more detailed information and resource pack for longer projects or if you are offering the same 'off-the-peg' workshop to several schools.

This pack should include most of the general information listed above, plus some detailed information about the specific approaches and resources you will be using in this project, including:

- information about the specific arts skills and processes you will be applying during the project, with a description of basic techniques

- background information on the art form(s) involved, including a brief history and references for books and other source material

- samples of any resources you intend to use during the project (e.g. a tape of music, book extracts)

- if the work is issue-based, background on the issue(s) and references for further reading

- ideas for preparatory and follow-up work (particularly important for issue-based work)

- resources, such as worksheets, which teachers can use with their pupils

- contact details for relevant organisations and suppliers.

Negotiating the terms of the project

You may have a clear idea of the project you would like to undertake, or be in the position of responding to a school's project. In either case you should be prepared to negotiate the terms of the project, to ensure that it is suitable for both yourself and the school.

A few artists have told us of bad experiences they have had after talking through project ideas with schools. They discussed their ideas in some detail with teachers, only to find that the school went ahead with the project without employing them. It is wise to be aware of this possibility when discussing your thoughts on a project with schools (get a firm commitment from the school before giving them all your ideas).

Project ideas

Some artists approach schools with their own ideas for artists-in-schools projects. This can be a good strategy, but designing your own project is likely to affect your relationship with schools. You will probably be expected to take a lead role in the development and organisation of the project. For example, teachers may expect you to take responsibility for raising money for the project.

If you decide to offer a specific project to schools, then you will need a clear concept of the project you have in mind. You could use the list of questions for putting together a project brief on page 41 as a basis for clarifying your thinking.

Artist-led projects are usually driven by a strong artistic vision, but just as an artist will want to negotiate on the artistic aspects of a school-initiated

project, you should expect teachers to negotiate with you to ensure that your project idea meets their pupils' educational needs.

Direct funding is rarely available to artists wishing to undertake artists-in-schools work. Grants are usually made to the school, which then pays the artist, or to an arts agency/organisation which acts as a broker between school and artist. Fundraising for a project would therefore usually need to be done in partnership with a school or agency.

See 'Funding your project' on pages 45 – 8.

Interviews

If you answer an advertisement, or if a school makes contact with you about a project, you should expect to see some kind of project brief (see page 42). You may be asked to attend an interview: although this is an opportunity for the school to assess your suitability for the project, you should have the chance to ask some questions of your own.

The questions you may wish to ask schools are listed on the following page.

The questions schools are likely to ask you are listed on pages 52 – 3.

Questions for artists to ask teachers

Experience

1. How did the idea for this project come about?

2. Has this school worked with professional artists before?

   Check:

   - Do these teachers have realistic expectations of what the project can achieve?

   - If this is the school's first involvement with artists, be prepared to explain how they can use you to best effect.

   - If this is not their first experience of working with artists, check how the teachers' experiences with other artists have shaped their expectations of this project.

Motivation and commitment

3. Why do you want a professional artist to visit your school?

4. Who will coordinate the project in the school?

5. Which members of staff will be directly involved?

6. Will anyone from outside the school be involved?

   Check:

   - Is there a shared understanding of the project among the people at the meeting?

   - Are all the key players at the meeting? Are they committed to the project?

   - Does the project have support from the top (e.g. from governors/headteacher/head of department)?

   - Would you be able to refer any areas of conflict to someone outside the school?

The work

7. How does this project fit in with your usual approach to teaching this part of the curriculum?

8. May I see some examples of the pupils' work?

   Check:

   - Will this project be supported within the school?

   - What are the parallels between your work and the existing curriculum?

Approach

9. What kind of experiences would you like me to offer to the pupils?

10. How do you envisage me working with pupils (classes, groups, individuals)?

11. Roughly how many pupils would be involved in total, and how many would I be working with at any one time?

12. How will teachers be involved (will a teacher be present during all work with the class)?

Check:

- In what ways is the school's approach similar to/different from your way of working?
- Are you happy to work with pupils in this way?
- Is the proposed number of pupils acceptable; and is it appropriate for the planned activities?
- How will teachers support your work with pupils?

Essential checks

- Discuss the budget: are the fees acceptable for the work involved?
- Ask about progress in securing funding.
- Check safety and insurance (see pages 29 – 30).
- Use this meeting to assess the school (look for evidence of a well-organised project; commitment, flexibility, and a compatible approach).

Taking a booking

Once a school has confirmed that they would like you to work with them, it is time to reach an initial agreement. You should be prepared to take a provisional booking from the school, providing that there is a specific date by which a firm decision will be reached. You can agree a cancellation fee in case either you or the school is unable to proceed with a definite booking when the deadline is reached (for example, if it has not been possible to raise the necessary funding for the project). This should be clarified when a provisional booking is made.

If the funding for the project has been secured, you may wish to sign a contract at this point.

(See Chapter 4, page 66 – 8).

Checklist:
an artist's guide to getting started

A good way of getting started is to consider the following:

✔ decide what you have to offer schools and what type(s) of involvement would suit you best

✔ find out more about the education system and the school curriculum

✔ get some relevant experience and/or training

✔ think about how to establish a good relationship with pupils

✔ check that your working practices are safe and obtain advice on appropriate insurance

✔ decide what to charge

✔ use local networks to find out about work opportunities

✔ get yourself listed on the relevant databases

✔ consider contacting schools direct

✔ prepare some publicity material

✔ put together an information pack

✔ prepare some questions to ask at interview

✔ if a school agrees to go ahead, accept a provisional booking from them.

a teacher's guide to getting started ③

This chapter focuses on the practical aspects of designing an artists-in-schools project, including:

- where you can get some information and advice
- the project brief
- the project budget
- funding your project
- safety
- finding artists
- choosing an artist
- making a booking.

Where to get information and advice

An artists-in-schools project can start in one of three ways. The idea can originate from within a school, from an artist, or from a third party (e.g. an LEA adviser or an agency which organises artists-in-schools work). In each case, it is important to ensure that the project fulfils a school's need for action, and that the school and artist are well informed about each other.

Before making any major decisions about a project, you may need to find out more about artists-in-schools work in general. This book will help to give you an overall picture, but you will also need more specific advice about what might be available to your school.

The most useful sources of information and advice for teachers are:

- other teachers who have experience of working with professional artists
- LEA advisers and advisory teachers
- local authority arts officers
- Regional Arts Boards (in England) and National Arts Councils (elsewhere in the UK)
- art form specific teachers' associations (e.g. the National Dance Teachers Association)
- artists' organisations, arts organisations and arts agencies.

See pages 97 – 100 for a listing of the main national, regional and local contact organisations.

Projects which are offered to you

It may be that you are offered the opportunity to take part in an artists-in-schools project by someone from outside the school (e.g. a local authority arts officer or a local arts organisation). Many arts organisations, such as theatres, museums and art galleries, have education programmes which offer schools opportunities to work with professional artists. Typically, this is in association with a performance, screening or exhibition at a local venue.

If the idea for a project has come from outside the school, you will need some detailed information about it. Some of the questions to ask are listed below.

- What is the purpose of the proposed involvement with schools?
- Do schools have to accept the project as it stands, or can we suggest changes?
- Has an artist already been selected for the project? (If so, is it possible for us to contact the artist direct to discuss his or her work and thoughts about the proposed project?)
- If an artist has not been selected, how will he or she be chosen?
- Who will be responsible for securing funding and drawing up a budget?

Once you have obtained the necessary information, try to make sure that everyone at your school who will be involved in the project is consulted. If, after this process of consultation, you feel that the project could meet a school need and would be suitable for the school, you should go ahead. If you have doubts which cannot be resolved through negotiation, it makes sense to turn down this particular project and to consider alternatives, such as designing one of your own.

Sometimes schools are offered one-off events or workshops which have been agreed between the artist/company and a host organisation (e.g. an arts centre), with little room for schools to negotiate the content of what is on offer. If you decide to take part in one of these events, it is a good idea to provide your contact at the arts organisation with some information about the pupils involved, so that they can pass this on to the artist/company. If the artist/company running the event has some information about the experience and ability level of your pupils, they should be able to ensure that the content and pacing is at an appropriate level.

Projects you design yourself

If the idea for an artists-in-schools project has originated in the school, it may be in response to a clear area of need (e.g. curriculum development) which you feel an artist could help you to address. Alternatively, a project could start from the desire to give pupils the opportunity to come into contact with professional artists. If this is your starting point, your next step is to consider which area(s) of the curriculum you would like the project to focus on and what type of involvement you would like an artist to have. Discuss your initial ideas with your colleagues. Once you have a clearer concept of what you want, you can find out more about what is available to schools in your area.

If you are new to this kind of work, you could find it helpful to talk through your ideas with someone who has had experience of organising an artists-in-schools project. It may be possible to get hold of an evaluation report on a similar project, or to speak to one of the people involved. You might need some advice on drawing up a project budget (see page 42), making funding applications (page 45) and contacting artists (page 49). When looking for advice, your LEA arts adviser or RAB education officer are good people to contact.

It is sensible for teachers planning their first artists-in-schools project to start with a shorter project (e.g. one or two days). You will then gain some experience of what artists can offer and will be in a better position to plan a more ambitious project in future.

When considering project ideas, you may find it helpful to refer to the features of successful projects described in Chapter 1, page 16.

Starting points for schools

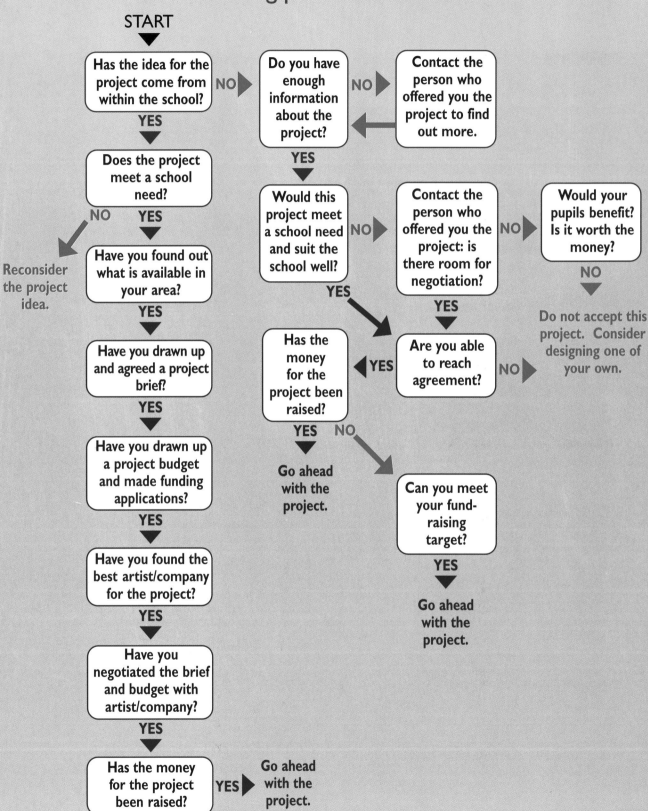

START

Has the idea for the project come from within the school? — **NO** → Do you have enough information about the project? — **NO** → Contact the person who offered you the project to find out more.

YES ↓

Does the project meet a school need? — **NO** → Reconsider the project idea.

YES ↓

Have you found out what is available in your area?

YES ↓

Have you drawn up and agreed a project brief?

YES ↓

Have you drawn up a project budget and made funding applications?

YES ↓

Have you found the best artist/company for the project?

YES ↓

Have you negotiated the brief and budget with artist/company?

YES ↓

Has the money for the project been raised? — **YES** → Go ahead with the project.

Do you have enough information about the project? **YES** ↓

Would this project meet a school need and suit the school well? — **NO** → Contact the person who offered you the project: is there room for negotiation? — **NO** → Would your pupils benefit? Is it worth the money?

NO ↓ (pupils benefit)

Do not accept this project. Consider designing one of your own.

YES (would this project) ↓

Contact the person... **YES** ↓ Are you able to reach agreement? — **NO** → Do not accept this project. Consider designing one of your own.

Has the money for the project been raised? ← **YES** — Are you able to reach agreement?

YES ↓

Go ahead with the project.

NO → Can you meet your fund-raising target?

YES ↓

Go ahead with the project.

Sample: questions on which to base the project brief

1. What is the main purpose of the project?

2. Which art form(s) will be involved?

3. What type of involvement will an artist or company have
   (e.g. presenting work and facilitating in practical sessions with pupils)?

4. Which members of school staff will be involved?

5. Who will take responsibility for coordinating the project?

6. Which pupils will be involved (age-group and approximate number)?

7. When will the project take place (proposed duration and approximate dates)?

8. How much time will the artist spend in the school, and how will their time be structured
   (e.g. one day INSET, followed by six days spread over a half term)?

9. How will the project be funded?

10. How will the project be evaluated?

The project brief

A written project brief helps to clarify the purpose and the 'shape' of the project, so that everyone taking part can get an idea of what will be involved. This will provide the basis for your initial thinking and for selecting an artist. Drawing up a brief is the responsibility of the person(s) designing the project, whether this is a teacher, an artist, or a third party.

The brief is a rough sketch of the project which provides a basis for negotiation by the school and the artist. It should include a statement about the purpose of the project and how an artist would be involved in the school. The details should not be finalised until both artist and teachers have discussed the project. However, some indication under each of the questions listed on page 41 will provide a useful basis for discussion.

In-service training

You may wish to hold an in-service training session to help teachers get to know the artist and his or her work. A preparatory session is particularly appropriate for projects aiming to introduce new art-form areas, issues, or ways of working which will be built into the curriculum after the project has ended. One way of tackling an introductory session is to plan a practical workshop, where teachers can experience a version of the work intended for pupils (but adapted for adults). The session should also include the following:

- an opportunity for teachers to talk about their experience of the training

- discussion about the proposed project, with some room for negotiation

- an opportunity for teachers to plan how they could best prepare for, support and follow up the project.

You could also consider holding INSET sessions during the project, perhaps as a means of enabling teachers who are not directly involved in the project to work with the artist. If you are considering including an INSET element, this will require specific negotiation with the artist who will need briefing about its purpose and his or her role.

Budgeting for the project

Drawing up the budget is usually done by the school. You will need a firm budget to raise funding, and so you may have to make decisions before you have selected an artist/company. However, you should be prepared to negotiate and agree the details with the artist at a later date. The main items to include in a project budget are as follows.

Artists' fees

Fees can vary according to the experience of artists and how popular they are.

- There are recommended minimum daily or sessional rates for artists working in schools. Contact your National Arts Council or English Regional Arts Board for details of the 'going rate'.

- Include payment for contributing to in-service events and attending project meetings, as well as for contact time with pupils.

Staff costs

- It is important to enable teachers to attend planning, review and feedback meetings. It may therefore be necessary to budget for staff cover to release the project coordinator and other members of staff to take part.

Travel and subsistence

This includes the artist's travel to and from the school, as well as any travel directly connected with the project.

- Artists should be paid expenses for attending selection interviews.

- If the artist lives some distance from the school, an allowance for overnight accommodation and meals may be required (although it is common practice for artists to stay with teachers during a project).

- Include any journeys by artists, staff and pupils which are directly connected with the project, such as travel to collect materials or equipment, and visits to other venues (e.g. studios, theatres, galleries and exhibition spaces).

Other expenses

These will vary according to the type of project being planned.

- Although it may be possible to use materials and equipment already in the school, some additional expenditure is usually required. (See also pages 64 – 5.)

- Include costings for an end-of-project display or performance, e.g. hire of a venue, publicity (posters and leaflets).

- Budget for sundries, such as: telephone calls, photocopying, postage and refreshments.

- Include an amount to cover evaluation costs (e.g. photocopying response sheets, photographs or video; printing of an evaluation report).

- Schools may wish to commission an artist to make a piece of art for the school.

- Additional insurance cover may be required.

- Include advertising costs, if relevant.

- It is good practice to include an amount for contingency — five per cent of the total budget would be appropriate for most projects.

Sample budget: Brockleton Secondary School

This sample budget is designed for a fairly large-scale residency, including an INSET course. Although we have tried to be realistic about the costs involved, we do not wish to imply that schools with a more limited budget cannot afford artists-in-schools projects.

Expenditure

	£
Artist's fees for:	
2x6-hour INSET sessions @ £120 a day	240.00
4x3-hour half day sessions @ £70 a session	280.00
2x2-hour planning meetings @ £35 a meeting	70.00
Artist's travel:	
2x return journeys by rail from home	80.00
Subsistence allowance @ £5.00 a day (5 days)	25.00
Supply cover	100.00
Materials for INSET and work with students	100.00
Printing of posters and programmes	40.00
Contingency (5 per cent of total budget)	41.75
Total expenditure	**976.75**

Projected income

Charitable trust grant	350.00
School INSET budget	150.00
School fundraising	100.00
Departmental budget allocation	150.00
Local business sponsorship	100.00
Programme advertising	25.00
Box office income (from public performance)	110.00
Total income	**985.00**
Projected surplus	**8.25**

Notes:

1. The artist's fees include an allowance for preparation.
2. Overnight accommodation and daily transport will be provided by Mrs Sharpe (Project Coordinator).

Funding your project

Artists-in-schools projects can be expensive, so you may need to raise additional money, particularly for more ambitious projects. This short section cannot tell you **how** to raise money, but it does provide some ideas to get you started.

There are many useful books on funding and fundraising, some of which are listed on pages 104 – 5.

Your fundraising strategy

The key to good fundraising is to devise a fundraising strategy which should include:

- a target amount
- a timescale with a deadline for raising your target amount
- a list of strategies for raising the money
- a fallback position should you fail or only partially succeed.

You may find it helpful to identify who is to take responsibility for fundraising. This could be one person or, if you are trying to raise quite a lot of money, a small committee (e.g. including a governor, the person coordinating the project, a representative from the Parent-Teacher Association and a community representative).

Your strategy could include the following:

- seeking funding from the school budget
- fundraising activity in the school
- securing local community support
- looking for funding 'in kind'
- applying to external funders.

School funding and fundraising

Once you have a clear idea about the project, it should be possible to identify relevant areas of the school budget (e.g. departmental funding, course-related funding, the INSET budget) from which you could obtain some funds. You may also consider some specific fundraising activity in the school (e.g. involving the pupils who will take part in the project, and/or the Parent-Teacher Association).

Securing local community support

Local community support for your project is extremely valuable. Many funders look for evidence of community support (and sometimes involvement) when considering grant applications. It also helps with publicity: for example, the local newspaper/ radio station is far more likely to be interested in the project if it has community backing.

Funding 'in kind'

Parents, governors and local businesses may be in a position to provide financial support in kind through discounted or free goods and services, including:

- materials
- equipment
- scrap materials
- accommodation and subsistence
- services — for example graphics and printing.

Applying to external funders

Applying to funders will be more successful if you:

- identify a number of potential funders
- assess their funding programmes, priorities and criteria
- try to find something in your project which will appeal to them and qualifies for funding against these criteria

- do not compromise your aims just to obtain money, but are realistic about what it is possible to raise money for.

Potential funders

You may consider applying to one or more of the following:

- artists-in-schools schemes
- local authority budgets
- National Lottery funding
- charitable trusts and foundations
- commercial sponsors
- development organisations and Training and Enterprise Council programmes
- European funding schemes.

Artists-in-schools schemes

These are generally funded by the Regional Arts Boards (RABs) in England and the National Arts Councils covering the rest of the UK.

At the time of writing, half the RABs fund artists-in-schools projects through schemes to which schools (and in one case artists/arts organisations) can apply. These schemes tend to give priority to projects in which clusters or groups of schools intend to work together, and to projects aiming to achieve long-term development. The RAB usually supports up to 50 per cent of the artist's fee, or provides a grant towards the total cost of the project up to a maximum amount/percentage.

Most of the RABs work closely with the local education authorities in their region and may have a partnership agreement with them. For example, one RAB has developed artists-in-education coordinator posts with several of its LEAs; another is establishing an independent arts education agency part-funded by an LEA which will be responsible for the funding and development of artists-in-schools projects in its area.

The three RABs covering the north of England have established the *Northern Artists into Schools Agency* and most of the funding for artists-in-schools work in these regions is directed through this agency.

Wherever you live, it is worth contacting your National Arts Council or RAB for information about its direct or indirect funding of artists-in-schools work. These organisations can offer information and advice to both schools and artists on artists-in-schools work, and some have publications and resources which could assist in the planning and evaluation of your project.

For information on how to contact the National Arts Councils and RABs, see pages 97 – 9.

Local authorities

Few of the English and Welsh LEAs have central funding for projects unless they are working in partnership with another agency, such as an RAB. However, it is worth contacting the relevant subject adviser or advisory teacher for information about your LEA's policy.

- If your project will result in improvements to school grounds and premises (e.g. through a commissioned piece of art), you may qualify for a grant from the school premises section.
- If your project involves the participation of young people outside normal school time, or includes parents in some of the sessions, you may be able to access money from the community education budget (e.g. through the Youth Service).

Other local authority departments which may be able to support artists-in-schools activity are those responsible for: arts and libraries; leisure; social services; and other specialist departments. Their interest will obviously depend on the aims and content of your project. Some local authorities have amalgamated their arts/leisure/tourism and education departments and most local authority arts and leisure strategies now include education as part of their brief. If you live in one of the English counties, you may find that you have a district arts officer **and** a county arts officer. They will both be interested in arts education and they both operate budgets.

● Contact your local authority arts officer(s) and any local councillors who may be supportive of the project.

National Lottery funding

Until very recently, National Lottery funding for the arts has been available for capital projects only. As we go to print, the Arts Council of England has just launched a scheme called *Arts for Everyone*, which for the first time enables organisations and groups to apply for Lottery funding for a wide range of arts projects, including artists-in-residence. Schools are eligible to apply for funding, although projects must be additional to statutory provision. Although individual schools can apply, the scheme encourages bids from clusters of schools.

The scheme is a pilot, and its future is dependent on central government decisions about how Lottery money is allocated.

● Contact your LEA arts adviser, RAB or National Arts Council for current information about the *Arts for Everyone* scheme.

Charitable trusts and foundations

Trusts and foundations are major sources of funding for artists-in-schools work, so it is worth taking the time and trouble to identify ones that may be interested in your project. Some trusts and

foundations operate nationally; others only fund work taking place in a particular geographical area.

● Get hold of one of the guides which detail the policies and criteria of trusts and foundations and target those which are most likely to fund your project (see pages 104 – 5).

Commercial sponsors

Some of the larger, national companies run arts education sponsorship programmes and schemes. You could target national companies which have local branches — e.g. supermarkets and chain stores, banks and manufacturing companies.

Even if a business does not have a donations policy or programme, it may well be willing to pay for advertising in a programme or exhibition catalogue. If you intend to approach local companies, remember that although they may give for philanthropic reasons, they will probably consider your application more favourably if they can see tangible benefits to their business, such as publicity.

● Use all the contacts you have, especially parents and governors, to interest local businesses in your project. The local Round Table, Chamber of Commerce or Rotary Club are good places to start.

ABSA

The Association for Business Sponsorship of the Arts (ABSA) is an agency responsible for promoting partnerships between the private sector and the arts. ABSA runs the *Pairing Scheme,* which makes awards to business sponsors of arts initiatives, including arts education projects. The scheme aims to encourage first-time sponsors of the arts, and to encourage existing funders to increase their sponsorship. ABSA matches a percentage of the sponsor's investment in the project, depending on the length of time the business has been an active sponsor. So, if you manage to persuade a new business sponsor to commit funding to your project, you could add extra value to their contribution by applying to ABSA.

- For further details of ABSA's *Pairing Scheme*, contact ABSA (see page 98).

Development organisations

If you live in an area covered by a Development Corporation or the Rural Development Commission, it may be worth contacting them for information about their funding programmes.

Artist-in-schools projects which have an emphasis on learning about the world of work may be of interest to your local authority Education Business Partnership Officer or to the local Training and Enterprise Council.

European funding

There is a wide range of European funding schemes which are aimed at the economic and social regeneration of deprived areas (city, urban, or rural). Many only consider funding artists-in-schools activity if it is part of a bigger project which has clear benefits for people outside the school.

- Contact your regional government office or your local authority's European Funding Officer.

Ensuring safety

Professional artists are in the same legal position as other visitors who work with pupils, such as instrumental music tutors. Schools are responsible for ensuring that pupils are protected from inappropriate behaviour on the part of all adults working in the school. It is the duty of both teachers and artists to make sure that the artist's working practices are safe, especially where pupils are concerned. The safety of the artist and the artist's property is another issue that needs to be considered.

Protection from child abuse

Everyone who works in education has become acutely aware of their duty to protect children from possible harm by staff or visitors to the school.

In the vast majority of cases, contact between artists and pupils will not provide opportunities for potential abuse. There is most cause for concern when an adult has substantial unsupervised access to children under the age of 16 (or 18, in the case of young people with special educational needs). Guidance on this issue is provided by the DFEE (see reference on page 104).

- The school should ask the artist for the name of a contact who can provide a character reference (preferably someone who can comment on the artist's suitability for working with children).

- Schools should avoid putting an artist into regular contact with individual children without supervision.

- It may be possible to check whether the artist has a conviction for a sexual offence.

Potential hazards

Issues of safety are most likely to arise when an artist is working with larger groups of young people, and during potentially hazardous activities (e.g. physical activities, or working with potentially harmful tools, equipment and materials). Safety is also an issue if visits to artists' studios or other venues are planned.

- You should discuss the artist's work with him or her in sufficient detail to identify any potential dangers to pupils.

- You should stay in the room to supervise the pupils whenever possible.

- If you delegate responsibility for pupils to an artist, you must be satisfied that the artist is capable of safeguarding the pupils, and you should check from time to time that the work is being carried out safely.

- If a visit to an artist's workplace is planned, you should discuss safety and insurance with the artist.

Example

A sculptor is working in a school with a group of children, helping them to make their own sculptures. The teacher has left the artist 'in charge' of the group while she works with the rest of the class in another room. Suddenly an accident occurs — a pupil injures herself with one of the artist's chisels. Who would be held responsible if the girl's parents took legal action?

In this hypothetical case, some of the possible outcomes are as follows:

- The teacher could be held to be negligent for not making sure that the artist's practices were safe before 'delegating' responsibility to him.

- The artist could be held responsible for allowing the pupil to use the chisel, especially if he had allowed her to use it in a dangerous manner.

- The governing body could be held liable too, for allowing the artist to work on the school premises without closer supervision.

Insurance

If an artist is self-employed, it is his or her responsibility to arrange and pay for appropriate public liability insurance. It is possible that the school's insurance may cover this, even if the artist is self-employed. If the artist is to be considered an employee, then it is the school's responsibility to arrange for appropriate insurance.

- Check the artist's employee status and the school's insurance cover (and obtain extra insurance if necessary).

- Check that the artist has taken out his or her own insurance, as necessary.

- Teachers and artists should make sure that the artist's property is safeguarded and insured while in the school. This is particularly important where an artist brings expensive equipment or valuable pieces of art into the school.

Finding artists for your project

Before you set about finding an artist for your project, you will need an outline of the kind of involvement you would like an artist to have (see pages 41 – 2, which give guidance on drawing up a project brief).

Make sure you have some flexibility so you can capitalise on what a particular artist has to offer. You should expect to negotiate the terms of the project with the artist concerned before a commitment is made. (Your LEA's personnel staff may be able to advise you on recruitment issues.)

Although you could work with an artist from anywhere in the country, it is worth considering whether there are artists living locally who would be suitable. Working with local artists has several advantages:

- minimal travel and subsistence expenses

- the opportunity to develop an ongoing relationship

- the possibility of visiting an artist in his/her workplace

- the ability to stress the local/regional interest to local press and sponsors.

You may wish to discuss the project with more than one artist before you reach a final decision. The three main methods which schools can use to contact artists are: personal recommendations; artist databases; and advertising.

Personal recommendations

Someone you know may be able to recommend an artist or company. This can be a useful starting point, but make sure that the recommended artist will meet the specific needs of your project.

Artist databases

Most of the National Arts Councils and RABs have databases of professional artists and companies who are available to visit schools in their area, or they can put you in touch with an agency which holds a database. There are some arts education agencies which offer a 'matching' service to schools, using their own databases. They will try to find a suitable artist for you, although most charge a small administrative fee for this service.

Some LEAs maintain databases, as do many local authority arts officers, and some arts organisations. There are also national and regional slide/image libraries, which contain examples of artists' work.

Databases are a means for artists to advertise their interest in working in schools. They are not usually

compiled by recommendation, so schools cannot make any assumptions about the quality of the artists' work or their suitability for working in schools.

Information held on each database varies, but will usually include:

- details of the artist or company's background and their work

- their experience in schools, any relevant training and their preferred way of working

- the names of referees (e.g. contacts in schools in which artists have worked).

See pages 97 – 9 for information on how to contact national and regional arts organisations.

Advertising

If you are planning a longer-term residency, you could consider advertising for artists, particularly if you need to find someone with very specific skills and experience. If you decide to advertise, you will need to budget for advertising costs. Consider where it would be best to advertise (e.g. specialist art-form publication, local press) and how you will select the successful applicant. Allow sufficient time for placing the advertisement, sifting through applications and interviewing.

Choosing an artist

You may have a shortlist of three or four artists, or just one you feel sure will fit the bill. Either way, it is essential that you interview the artist(s) before booking them, even if this has to be done by telephone.

Although the school will be employing the artist, the project should be based on a partnership between artist and teachers. It is helpful if the selection process is viewed as one of negotiation, and includes time for both sides to ask questions and engage in discussion. Artists and teachers should treat this as an opportunity to explore the idea of working together — either side should feel free to withdraw if agreement cannot be reached.

For longer-term residencies, a face-to-face interview is essential and should involve:

- the person responsible for coordinating the project in the school

- the artist (or company representative)

- at least one of the teachers who would be involved with the project.

It may also be appropriate to invite an LEA adviser to the interview and/or a major funder (if you have one).

Before the interview, send the artist(s) a copy of the project brief, which should form the basis of your discussion. At the same time, you could ask the artists to provide examples of their recent work (if the work is unsuitable for portfolio presentation, you should expect to see photographs and reviews, or perhaps a video).

Once a decision has been reached and you have agreed to work together, you will need to discuss the project brief in detail and agree changes, if necessary.

Some funders and sponsors will not commit money until there is a named artist working on a project. However, most funders will outline their funding criteria to you and be prepared to give you an indication of the likelihood of their support before this stage is reached.

Questions for teachers to ask artists

Here is a list of questions and points to check during an interview. The questions which artists are likely to ask you are listed on pages 34 – 5.

Training and experience

1. Can you tell us a bit about your training as an artist?

2. Have you had any specific training to work in schools?

3. Have you had any experience of working with young people?

4. Have you had any experience of working on projects similar to this one?

   If yes

   a) What kind of settings have you worked in (e.g. school, youth club)?

   b) What was your most recent project about?

   c) What worked well? What didn't work so well? Why?

   If no

   d) Have you worked with adults in an educational or community project?

   Check:

   - What are the points of similarity and difference between the artist's previous experience and this project/school?

   - Has the artist encountered any particular difficulties working in schools?

   - If this artist has not worked in schools before, can they demonstrate the ability to communicate their practice to your pupils?

   - Does the artist have an understanding of the constraints of working in schools?

Motivation and commitment

5. Why do you want to work in schools?

6. Why do you want to be involved with this particular project?

   Check:

   - Would this person be motivated and committed to your project?

The work

7. (If not seen in advance) Can we see some examples of your recent work?

8. How might your work be a stimulus or model for work with our pupils?

9. Would you envisage our pupils producing similar work or using similar techniques?

Check:

● Is the work of good quality?

● Do you like the artist's work? How do you think your pupils would respond?

● Assess the suitability of the work for the pupils who will be involved in the project.

● What are the parallels between the artist's work and the existing curriculum?

● Does the artist's work provide opportunities for curriculum development that teachers could explore within the project?

Approach

10. How do you envisage working with pupils? (Are you happy addressing large groups, or do you prefer working with small groups or individuals?)

11. What kind of activities would you suggest for the pupils? (What would pupils actually do?)

Check:

● How much opportunity would pupils have for expressing their own ideas?

● In what ways is the artist's approach similar to/different from that of the teachers?

● What implications does this have for the role of the teachers?

Essential checks

● Discuss the budget: are the fees acceptable to the artist; are there any items to add?

● Check safety and insurance (see pages 48 – 9).

● Use this meeting to assess the artist's suitability for working in your school (look for evidence of high-quality work, commitment, flexibility, a compatible approach and good communication skills).

3

a teacher's guide to getting started

Making a booking

Once an artist/company has been selected for a project, it is time to reach an initial agreement. Artists and companies should be prepared to accept a provisional booking, providing that there is a specific date by which a firm decision will be reached. If either side does not wish to proceed with a definite booking when the deadline is reached (for example, if it has not been possible to raise the necessary funding for the project), a cancellation fee may be required. This should be clarified when a provisional booking is made.

If the funding for the project has been secured, you may wish to sign a contract at this point (See Chapter 4, pages 66 – 8).

Checklist:
a teacher's guide to getting started

A good way of getting started is as follows:

✔ consider any projects you are offered, looking for room for negotiation

or

✔ design you own project.

If you design your own project, here are some actions to consider:

✔ discuss initial ideas and get some advice

✔ write a project brief

✔ draw up a project budget and make funding applications

✔ contact suitable artists/companies

✔ think about safety and obtain appropriate insurance

✔ interview and choose an artist/company

✔ make a provisional booking with them.

This chapter is in three main sections.

School planning

- Project coordination.
- Setting aims, objectives and success criteria.
- Selecting pupils.
- Creating a context for the work.
- Preparing pupils.
- Informing others.
- Practical arrangements.

Teachers and artists planning together

- Clarifying and agreeing aims and objectives.
- Planning content and structure.
- Planning the work with pupils
- Defining roles.
- Discussing evaluation.
- Discussing practicalities, such as the workspace, materials and equipment.
- Agreeing the project plan.
- Contracts.

Artists' planning

- Preparing for working with pupils.
- Preparing to meet pupils' learning needs (including pupils with special needs).
- Planning an introductory talk.

The chapter offers a framework to lead teachers and artists through the process of planning an artists-in-schools project. It assumes that the project idea started from within the school or at least that the school has the major responsibility for its planning. However, this chapter is designed to help any school, artist or company participating in an artists-in-schools project to maximise the potential of their joint involvement.

If artists and teachers are to work together then it makes sense to plan together. The school will usually have the main responsibility for planning, but it should be done in partnership with the artist wherever possible. Artists and teachers need to develop a mutual, professional understanding and it is during the planning phase that such an understanding can be established.

School planning

The guidance for this stage is primarily for teachers and addresses them directly. However, artists may find it useful to read the section on aims and objectives (pages 56 – 8), and on selecting pupils (pages 58 – 9) as it will help when they plan with the school. The section on joint planning starts on page 62.

Project coordination

If more than one teacher is involved in the project, it is essential that someone from within the school takes overall responsibility for its organisation. The project coordinator is often the person who initiated the project, but it may be appropriate for someone else to take on the role. The project coordinator may wish to involve other teachers in a small planning team.

Where more than one school is involved, there may be an 'external' project coordinator. This person could be an advisory teacher, an arts development officer, an education officer from an arts organisation or perhaps an animateur. The role of the external coordinator will be to help each school make decisions about how best to use the artist, and to facilitate discussion between schools.

Setting aims, objectives and success criteria

Once the decision has been made to go ahead with the project, you need to revisit the purpose of the project and develop it more fully into a list of aims and objectives. These can then form the basis for agreement with your selected artist/company.

● The aims should be broad statements of what you want the project to achieve.

● The objectives should express how the aims will be achieved and will help you to plan the activities for pupils to enable them to acquire the relevant skills, knowledge and understanding.

● The success criteria should provide clear and specific targets for judging the project's progress and longer-term success.

As we explained in Chapter 1, the experience of the teachers and artists who helped in the research showed that those taking part in a project need to identify, discuss and agree its aims and objectives. Participants can have differing expectations of a project and, if these are never aired, people can end up pulling in opposite directions.

Some of the teachers and artists who took part in the research were reluctant to set aims because they wanted to be free to experiment, to launch into a project and discover what was possible as they went along. Yet by avoiding setting any aims, they were running the risk that the purpose of the project would be confused and confusing to those taking part. It would also be difficult for these schools to plan for the project as part of their whole programme. One compromise in this situation might be to set aims which form a statement of intent, but which leave the outcomes open. For example, this type of aim might state: 'The project aims to enable pupils to experiment in the use of dance/movement as a form of expression for the pupils' own ideas.'

The aims and objectives provide a framework for the project. It is not, however, possible to anticipate fully all the outcomes of a project in advance. The aims and objectives are a useful guide but need not be followed rigidly: they may have to be adapted and changed as the project progresses.

Setting aims and objectives for your project

This should be done in consultation with other teachers and should be negotiated with the artist. We suggest the following process:

- set aims

- prioritise aims and set objectives

- identify success criteria

- negotiate and agree the aims, objectives and success criteria with the artist/company.

Set aims

You may find it helpful to look at the possible benefits of an artists-in-schools project described in Chapter 1. Which of these particularly appeals to you? Which would suit your pupils, teachers and the artist best? How could you express these clearly as aims for your project? Try to arrive at a small number of aims (e.g. two or three) as a basis for discussion.

Once you have decided what you want the project to achieve, check that:

- everyone understands what the aims mean

- they relate clearly to the original purpose of the project

- they are ambitious, but feasible, given the resources and time available

- taken together, they contain something for all participants (including the artist)

- the aims do not conflict with each other

- there is nothing missing that really should be included.

Prioritise aims and set objectives

You should now have your final list of aims. You may find it helpful to prioritise them (it can be useful to have an agreement about which aims are most important, in case you find it difficult to achieve all of them fully when the project gets under way).

When the provisional set of aims has been agreed, the next step is to work out some objectives which will shape the project and enable you to realise your aims. These could include targets for events during the project (e.g. holding a meeting by a specific date/ stage in the project).

Identify success criteria

The purpose of success criteria is to provide a set of tangible goals for participants. They should include a statement of the outcomes (e.g. the skills, knowledge and understanding that you intend pupils to achieve).

Setting success criteria will help you to monitor progress and evaluate the project (see also Chapter 6).

Negotiate and agree the aims with the artist

When you have defined your project's aims, objectives and success criteria, send them to the artist for approval/amendment. Once you have an agreed list, you are in a good position to move forward on deciding how to realise them through the planned inputs and activities.

Example

The head of the art department has raised funding for a project to broaden the cultural base of the art curriculum. The project is timed to coincide with an exhibition of art and artefacts from Africa at a local museum. The school has selected a visual artist who is African, but is currently living and working in the UK. He will be working with students in Year 8 and will accompany them on a visit to the museum exhibition. **One** of the project's aims is detailed below.

Aim

- To study examples of traditional and contemporary African art and to explore the relationship between them.

Objectives

- To show the influence of traditional African art and of contemporary forms in this artist's work, and to learn about his experience of working alongside other African artists.

- To develop students' knowledge and understanding of how artists are influenced by other artists.

- To enable students to create workbooks to record information and develop ideas.

- To give students the opportunity to practise working in the artist's style.

- To display and use information from the museum exhibition before and during the artist's visit.

- To evaluate the students' responses to the museum visit through response sheets and group discussion.

Success criteria

1. All students demonstrate an understanding of the main features of traditional and contemporary African arts practice in the examples from the exhibition and the artist's own work (as shown in students' workbooks and their comments during group discussion).

2. Some students demonstrate an understanding of the characteristics which are shared by the examples of traditional and contemporary African art.

Selecting pupils

When selecting the pupils who will take part in the project, it may be helpful to consider the following questions.

- Which pupils will make best use of the artist's presence?

- Which year group(s) would benefit most (e.g. how will the project fit with the curriculum; will certain year-groups have more time to participate)?

- Is the project for pupils who have never done this kind of work before, or is it for pupils who already have some skills in a specific area and need to develop them further?

- Should the group include young people with special needs?

- Should any potentially disruptive pupils be included?

- How many pupils should take part?

Some of these decisions may already have been made, but it could be helpful to revisit them in the light of the agreed aims and objectives.

Artists-in-schools projects are most likely to succeed when they are carefully targeted at pupils who will get the most out of the experience. This may suggest a particular year group or even particular personalities. Projects are often demanding of pupils and require a considerable commitment from them. This is not to say that projects should only involve pupils who already have a good track record of participation in school activities, as the following example illustrates.

Case study

An English teacher wanted her students to have the opportunity to work with a professional writer during his residency in the school. The project involved the students in one-to-one sessions with the writer, discussing their own pieces of writing. The work led to a compilation of written work for the school. The teacher put up posters inviting students to volunteer to take part but, in agreement with the writer, she also personally encouraged certain students to apply, including some who had low attainment, lacked self-esteem, and had a poor record of attendance.

Although not all of these students remained in the project, there were notable examples of success. Students who had felt alienated from the school became dedicated to the project and felt a great sense of achievement in their work. The teacher gave an example of one girl who had been truanting very badly. She became involved in the project and kept her appointments with the writer: 'Now she says she's sad to leave school because of her involvement with [the writer].'

Although teachers will probably take the main responsibility for pupil selection, the artist should be consulted about the criteria for selection and the resulting pupil group. There is also a need to check that the artist is happy to work with the estimated number of pupils, and that pupil numbers are appropriate for the proposed activities.

Having established a broad 'target group', the practical means of determining which pupils should participate need to be agreed. Whether it is best to let pupils volunteer to take part or to select them yourselves will depend on the project's purpose and the type of involvement the artist is to have.

Creating a context for the work

The research found that the most successful projects were those where schools established a meaningful context for the artist's work, and where artists responded to the needs of the school.

One of the key factors contributing to successful projects is to establish a curriculum context for the work. This is particularly important in the case of short-term involvements and projects aiming to explore new areas of the curriculum, both of which applied in the following example.

Case study

A group of three rural primary schools took part in a project aiming to explore multicultural issues by studying the Caribbean. As part of the project, they invited a Caribbean dancer to visit each school for one or two days. By the time the dancer arrived, the pupils had been studying the Caribbean for about half a term, and were already familiar with many aspects of the topic, including the history and geography of the Caribbean. Some members of staff had also attended a one-day INSET session with the dancer before they began to work on the topic with their classes.

After the project had ended, the teachers agreed that their preparatory work had made all the difference to the value the schools derived from the dancer's visit. As one teacher said: 'I knew some of the things he would be doing because I joined in that [in-service training] session with him. It helps to meet face-to-face and then the teacher can contribute more, prepare the children and develop it afterwards. I think the pupils would have responded well anyway, but it was far more valuable that the context was there. We got more out of it because *he* enhanced what *we* were doing.'

Preparing pupils

Pupils should be informed about the project's aims, how it will fit in with their previous work and what will be required of them. They will also need some information about the artist and his or her work.

It will normally be the teacher's responsibility to prepare the pupils who will be taking part in the project, but this should be discussed with the artist beforehand.

Artists should be able to provide one or more of the following:

- information about themselves and their work
- samples of their work
- examples of source material and preparatory work
- photographs of themselves at work
- reviews and press cuttings
- slides, audio or video recordings.

Photographs, slides and video recordings are particularly useful for preparatory work with the pupils directly involved in the project.

Preparing pupils with special educational needs

Teachers of pupils with special educational needs will have clear ideas about how to prepare their pupils for a new experience. Many teachers of pupils with learning difficulties who contributed to the research felt that it would be unhelpful to prepare pupils for an artist's visit too far in advance, because the pupils' short-term memory can be poor.

It may, however, be a good idea to do some practical arts preparation with the pupils to familiarise them with processes or elements of the work they will be doing with the artist. For example, by introducing some gentle warm-up exercises a few weeks prior to a dance/movement project with a professional dancer, a teacher could prepare pupils both mentally and physically. The dancer could then build on this by doing some of the same exercises with the pupils at the beginning of the first session. The familiarity of the exercises could help overcome any pupils' anxiety caused by working with someone they do not know.

Informing others

Artists-in-schools projects are more likely to have an impact in the school when the whole school is aware that the project is taking place. Consider using some of the following strategies.

- Produce an information sheet about the project for distribution to staff and pupils. This could consist of an outline of the project, a photograph of the artist and a short description of his or her work.

- Plan a display about the artist's visit. This could be mounted in the reception area of the school, where everyone will see it. Artists are usually willing to lend their work to schools, as long as the work is protected and adequate insurance cover is arranged.

- Inform parents by putting an item into a school newsletter and/or sending them a letter. If you would like parents to participate, include details of how they could contribute, and who to contact.

Parents' permission for their child to take part may have been sought already, in which case they will know something about the project. Parents and governors should continue to be informed about the project and its progress. Teachers and artists should decide together if they want the project publicised more widely at this stage (e.g. in the local press). However, it may be better to wait until the project is well under way and any initial problems have been dealt with.

Practical arrangements

Before the project is about to start, check that the following arrangements have been made.

- All the rooms are booked.

- If individual pupils are to be 'withdrawn' from normal lessons, this has been agreed with other teachers, and pupils have been told the rules for obtaining permission to miss lessons and copying up work.

- The coordinator is free to meet the artist on the first day.

- Staff cover arrangements have been made.

- Parents have been informed about the project.

- Pupils know they have to bring appropriate clothing.

- The necessary liaison with the caretaker and cleaners has taken place.

- The artist knows what time to be there, and how to find his or her way around the school. (Some information about the security system and a plan of the school will help.)

Teachers and artists planning together

This part of the planning process could take place during a planning meeting. If there is not enough time to hold a meeting, the artist should be consulted about all the key decisions by telephone.

For projects which have originated from a third party, teachers and artists must make sure that they have enough information to plan for the project. For a longer-term project, teachers and artists should ask to meet the person organising the project to discuss and agree the details.

Clarifying and agreeing aims and objectives

The artist should make sure that he or she understands the meaning of the aims and objectives outlined by the school and should explain his or her personal aims in undertaking the project. An artist may have a different view of what can be achieved through the project (particularly in relation to the artistic aims), and teachers should be willing to discuss possible adaptations to the aims. When the aims, objectives and success criteria have been agreed with the artist they can be circulated to everyone involved.

Planning content and structure

The activities should be planned at a reasonably detailed level, working towards agreement from all concerned about how to create a coherent set of experiences for teachers and pupils. The activities should be developed from the objectives, enabling pupils to acquire the necessary skills, knowledge and understanding to achieve the project's aims.

Inevitably, as the project's content is discussed, questions will arise about the best way to use the available time, and how to structure the project. The structure is the backbone of the project, giving it strength and support but being flexible enough to meet the changing demands made upon it. There is no ideal structure; it will depend on the project's aims and objectives, the type of involvement the artist is to have, and the time available.

The events around which most projects are structured are:

- a planning meeting between artist(s) and teachers
- an introductory session for the artist to meet participating pupils
- the main sessions forming the core of the project (i.e. the activities for pupils)
- review meeting(s) to discuss progress
- a performance, screening or exhibition, to celebrate the work of the project
- a final evaluation/feedback meeting.

Schools and artists may wish to include other activities, for example:

- sessions for the artist to work separately with teachers
- time between sessions for the artist to do his/ her own work (in or out of the school).

The artist's time is a major consideration: how many hours/days will the artist spend in the school and how can the time best be organised to use his or her contribution effectively? Two possible structures are given below.

A series of visits

If an artist is helping teachers to introduce a new art-form to the curriculum, it might be appropriate to make a 'sandwich' of the artist's sessions.

4

1. The artist first works with the teachers, helping them to build their own skills and confidence.

2. The artist begins a project with pupils.

3. The artist returns to work with pupils at intervals, allowing time for the teachers to develop the work in between visits.

It helps if the artist agrees to keep in contact with the coordinator during the period when he or she is not working with the pupils, to find out about progress and to provide support and guidance for teachers.

An intensive project

The artist's time can also be 'blocked' so that the artist spends an intensive period in the school. This would be an appropriate structure for a one-day visit or an 'arts week', for example.

Planning the work with pupils

Once a basic structure has been agreed for the activities, more specific questions about pupil contact and timetabling should be considered. Some of the questions which need to be asked about pupil contact are listed below.

- Which type of artist–pupil contact is most appropriate (i.e. will the artist be making, presenting, facilitating/instructing)?

- Is it important that all pupils have the same amount of contact time with the artist?

- Will the pupils involved be 'off timetable', or will the sessions form part of their normal timetable?

- Will the artist work with whole classes, smaller groups or individual pupils?

- If groups, how will they be organised (e.g. by age) and what is the optimum size for each group?

Defining roles

Artists and teachers need to establish how they will work together. Teachers and artists generally do have a different view of things and, if this is approached positively, it is one of the strengths of an artists-in-schools project.

The artist's role will depend on why he or she is in the school and on the type of pupil/teacher/artist contact this requires. If the artist is to take the role of instructor/facilitator with pupils, then the following points need to be considered.

- Who will take the main responsibility for planning the content and learning outcomes of the sessions?

- What is the artist's preferred way of working (e.g. leading a workshop session, demonstrating techniques to individuals or groups)?

- Who will take responsibility for classroom management? (While some artists have a natural authority and ability to maintain order, others find it difficult to do so, and would prefer not to take on this responsibility.)

If the group is to include pupils with special needs, or pupils who are potentially disruptive, artists and teachers should discuss what consequences this will have for the artist, and plan how school staff will support the participation of these pupils in the project. A joint strategy should be agreed for meeting the needs of individual pupils and dealing with any problems of disruption if they arise.

The teacher's role

Several of the teachers who took part in the research were worried about working with the artist because they thought they might 'cramp the artist's style'. If teachers and artists understand each other's perspective and ways of working, they should not find it difficult to develop a joint strategy for working together.

Decide whether the teacher or artist will take the lead during a session, or whether the teacher and artist will work together in a team-teaching situation.

It may be appropriate for the teacher to adopt the role of 'student', learning from the artist alongside the pupils.

Ideally a teacher should be present during all work with groups of pupils. If the artist is working on his or her own with small groups or individuals, the teacher needs to keep an eye open for any discipline problems or safety issues. Teachers should ask the artist for feedback before the artist's next session with the group (e.g. an outline of what happened and how the pupils responded). Artists should never be left in sole charge of a whole class or large group of pupils.

The pupils' roles

The role of the pupils themselves should be given some consideration. Artists-in-schools projects sometimes offer possibilities for pupils to take on new roles and responsibilities. Some of the questions you may wish to consider are:

How will the roles of pupils relate to those of artist and teachers?

Will all the pupils be expected to take part in the project in the same way?

How much choice will pupils have in deciding on key elements of the project, such as subject matter, materials and outcomes?

Discussing evaluation

Evaluation should be an integral part of any project, taking place both during the project and after it has finished. The success criteria will form a useful part of this process.

At the planning stage, it is important to decide how to evaluate the project and to build in sufficient time to do so.

Methods of evaluation are discussed in detail in Chapter 6.

Discussing practicalities

Teachers and artists should discuss where the artist will be working. Some artists have particular working requirements. For example, a theatre-in-education (TIE) or dance company will probably have a minimum requirement for the size of a performance area. Some visual artists or craftspeople may need easy access to running water, while a writer will probably want a quiet area in which to work.

When the workspace has been chosen, teachers and artists should work together on creating the right environment. It is important that the artist feels comfortable there and that the workspace should reflect something of the artist and his or her work

The artist should have the opportunity to visit the proposed workspace(s) before the project begins. If this is not possible, then the coordinator could describe the workspace to the artist over the telephone.

Consider mounting a display of the artist's work in the chosen space. Pupils' work could be displayed alongside that of the artist.

Materials and equipment

Teachers may suggest that they would like the artist to work with resources which would normally be available to them. Some teachers and artists positively welcome this approach, as it gives the artist's work a direct and visible link to that of the teachers. This, in turn, means that the teachers can more easily replicate or develop the work after the project has finished. However, teachers and artists need to discuss whether the proposed materials and equipment are suitable for the project, and clarify exactly what is required.

For a discussion of safety and insurance see pages 29 – 30 (artists) and 48 – 9 (teachers).

Case study

In one school, a visiting writer asked the teacher to provide some felt pens and paper for pupils to write on. When he arrived in the school, it became apparent that the pupils needed writing books or paper with clipboards so that they had something firm to write on, and that large felt pens were required so that the writing could be seen from a distance. As the teacher commented: 'When all the children are assembled for a precious workshop, it's too late to scrabble around for the right pens.'

One way of bringing in new resources at little cost is to use 'scrap' materials, which can be ideal for some art and craft work (set-building, props- and costume-making, for example). As we mentioned in Chapter 3, many local manufacturing companies have scrap or reject materials which they are willing to give away. Some local authorities run 'scrap banks' or projects which schools can join. Parents can also be a good source of scrap materials, and may be able to provide links with local firms.

- The artist may wish to oversee the ordering of specialist materials to ensure that the right ones are obtained. (This could be particularly important if the school has little or no previous experience of working with the materials.)

- If the school takes responsibility for obtaining materials, then the artist must be specific about the quantity and quality required.

- If school equipment is to be used, the artist should have the opportunity to make sure that it is suitable. It is the coordinator's responsibility to book equipment and to check to see that it is in good working order.

- If the artist intends to bring his or her own equipment to the school, insurance, health and safety may be at issue.

Agreeing the project plan

Once teachers and artists have agreed all the details, it is useful to expand the project brief into a fuller outline of the project.

The plan should provide details of:

- the aims, objectives and success criteria

- structure and content

- an outline timetable

- how the artist will be working in the school

- which members of staff are involved (and how)

- who is responsible for what

- which pupils are to be involved, including how they have been selected

- what resources will be involved (e.g. workspace, equipment and materials)

- how the project will be evaluated.

This will provide a summary of all the issues and practicalities that have been discussed during the planning stage.

Having an agreed plan is one way of minimising disagreements about decisions that were made during the project's planning. It provides a frame of reference for discussion during the project and heightens everyone's understanding of what the project is about.

Contracts

Once agreement has been reached between school and artist, and funding has been secured, it is time to make a firm booking and formalise the agreement in a written contract. A contract is important for both artists and schools: it clarifies the responsibilities of each 'partner'; sets down the conditions for payment of fees to the artist; and

offers protection in case either partner reneges on the agreement. A written contract provides a foundation for a good partnership between artist and school: you are strongly advised to use one.

Some funding bodies and artists' organisations can provide examples of contracts for artists and schools to use as models. See also recommended publications on page 103.

Sample contract notes

- The sample contract on pages 67 – 8 is provided as a general guide for artists and teachers. Those responsible for drawing up such contracts are advised to seek further advice (e.g. from an LEA, RAB/National Arts Council, or artists' organisation) especially where longer-term residencies are concerned.

- Do not enter into a contract unless the funding for the project has been secured.

- If artists find that the school/agent does not intend to issue a contract, it is open to them to draw up a contract for the school/agency to sign. Failing this, artists are advised to send a letter to the project coordinator, stating the agreed terms of the project. Send it by recorded mail to ensure proof of postage, and keep a copy in case of disputes.

- Some funders require the submission of an evaluation report within a certain period of the end of the project as a condition of their grant. If an evaluation report is an agreed part of the project, this should be acknowledged in the contract (point 7).

- If either the school or the artist feels that the terms of the contract have been broken, then they must inform the other party in writing, identifying the problem and requesting that action is taken to put it right within a specified period of time (see point 11). If agreement is reached, a statement acknowledging this can be signed by both parties and attached to the contract.

Sample Contract

This contract sets out the terms of agreement between

and

1. Project description

The project is described in the accompanying Project Plan, which has been agreed by both school and artist.

2. Funding

The project is to be funded by the following bodies:

The administration of the budget is the responsibility of:

3. Duration

The artist's work will commence on   and end on

The artist's work for the project will consist of the following activities/events and time allocations:

4. Fees

The school agrees to pay the artist fees for the residency totalling £
in the following instalments:

£   payable on completion of the first part of the work, by   (date).

£   payable on completion of the work, by   (date).

£   payable on submission of a written evaluation report, by   (date).

5. Expenses

The school agrees to pay the artist's project-related expenses as follows (evidence of payment will be required)

Travel

Materials

Accommodation

Subsistence

Other specified expenses

6. Facilities, equipment and materials

The following facilities, equipment and materials will be supplied by the school:

The following equipment and materials will be supplied by the artist:

7. Evaluation report

The artist and the school will each submit a report on the residency to

within   of completion of the project.

8. Insurance

Public liability insurance cover for the project will be obtained
and paid for by:

The insurance of the artist's property is the responsibility of:

9. Copyright

The artist owns the copyright of any work created by the artist during the project. Any work created jointly by the artist and pupils/teachers will be the joint copyright of all contributors.

The artist agrees to allow the school to reproduce any of his/her work created during the project for purposes directly connected with the project (e.g. publicity).

10. Unforeseen circumstances

If the project is delayed due to unforeseen circumstances (such as accident, sickness or bereavement) the parties agree to discuss the matter with a view to rescheduling the proposed project.

11. Cancellation and termination of contract

If either party cancels at short notice and is unwilling or unable to reschedule, a cancellation fee of £
will be paid to the other party. Either party may terminate this agreement if the other fails to abide by the terms, provided notice is given in writing, and the deficiency has not been rectified within

Signed (Artist)   Date

Signed (School representative)   Date

Artists' planning

This section is for artists and addresses them directly.

By the time the project is about to begin, you need to have sufficient knowledge of the school, and the teachers and pupils involved, to be able to prepare for working with them. Artists who are new to this kind of project should consider how best to communicate the skills and creative processes used in their work.

Preparing for working with pupils

The approach used for a particular project will depend on the project's aims and objectives, the type of contact with pupils, and on the age and number of the pupils taking part. For example, if pupils are to learn specific skills, then you need to consider how to communicate those skills clearly, simply and effectively. It may be that you will be working on a commission in consultation with staff and pupils: how will their comments and suggestions be included? It is here that discussion with the teachers is really useful; their expertise in planning work for pupils will help you to prepare for working in the school. It might also be appropriate to look at examples of pupils' work before the project begins (if your contribution is part of an ongoing project in the school, for instance).

When thinking about the first sessions, you may find it helpful to consider the following questions.

Content of each session

- How long will each session be?
- How will the session begin?
- What do you want to achieve by the end of the session (i.e. in relation to the project's aims and objectives)?

- How will pupils' individual learning needs be met?
- If progress is faster or slower than expected, how can the activities be cut/extended?
- How will the session end?

Organisation of the room

- Will the lay-out of the room need to be changed to suit the content of the session?
- What equipment and materials will be needed?
- Where will materials/equipment be placed, and who will set them up?

Grouping the pupils

- Will it be necessary to group pupils for all or part of the session?
- What size of groups will be best?
- How will groups be formed (friendship groups, single/mixed sex, etc.)?
- What will each group do (will everyone work on the same task)?

Roles

- Who will take responsibility for what within the session?

Both you and the teacher should be fully in the picture about plans for initial sessions. The approaches adopted at the beginning of the project can then be reviewed and adapted as the residency progresses.

Preparing to meet pupils' learning needs

Find out about the pupils you will be working with. Have they had any experience of working with artists? You will usually find that you are working with mixed-ability groups. What is the teachers' view of the ability levels of the pupils? Will there be any potentially disruptive pupils in the groups? Will there be pupils with special educational needs (SEN) in any of the groups? If so, you may need to think more carefully about the content of your sessions and your approach to the work. As we pointed out in the joint planning section, it is vital that you discuss the needs of these pupils in detail with the teacher(s) concerned and develop a joint strategy for working with them.

Preparing for work with pupils with special educational needs

It is important not to underestimate children with SEN: a child who has learning difficulties in language and number may not have learning difficulties in the arts. On the other hand, you need to be aware of what their limitations might be. For example, if a dancer was planning a session with pupils with SEN, he or she would need to know if there were any pupils with poor muscle control or other physical problems which might affect their participation. Many pupils with learning or behavioural difficulties have a short attention span; if this is the case, it is advisable to include several changes of focus within one session or performance. However, it is important not to overload the pupils, so try to concentrate on one thing at a time.

Language is another important consideration. Most children with moderate or severe learning difficulties have a limited vocabulary (although they may understand more words than they are able to use in their speech). This means that the language content (e.g. in a TIE programme) has to be

considered carefully. If you want pupils to discuss your work (or theirs), you will need to find ways of communicating and expressing concepts so that they understand what you are trying to say.

> ### Case study
>
> A weaver made a preliminary visit to a special school where the teacher used a non-verbal means of introducing the concept of weaving to the pupils. The weaver explained: 'I was invited to join in a circle while a pupil was chosen to trail ribbons round the back of the circle. This developed into a weaving process with longer and longer ribbons. The kids had lots of energy and it seemed a good thing to get started in this physical way. After break, we lined the children up in a row and I wove a trail of ribbons between each child so they got more and more enmeshed. They were enacting the warp threads and experienced for themselves the locking together that is created by the weaving in and out of the weft - in this case, the ribbon.'

More information on children with special educational needs is given in Chapter 2, page 27, and some books on the subject are listed on page 107.

Planning
an introductory talk

If you are planning to give an introductory talk at the beginning of the project, this too will require preparation.

- Find out about the audience for, time and location of, your talk.

- Be clear about the purpose of your talk. Decide what you want to say and why.

- Choose the examples of work, slides, etc. which will provide the best illustrations.

- Think about how to introduce complex ideas and explain any terms which may not be familiar to the pupils.

- Rehearse your talk several times (actually speak it out loud).

- Check the timing and remember to leave some time for questions.

- You may wish to make a few written notes (you can use index cards for this), but avoid reading out a written speech as this makes for a boring presentation.

- You may find it helpful to practise your talk in front of a friend, who could give you some constructive feedback. When you are fairly happy with the content, you could outline it to the coordinator and ask for comments.

- Ask for any equipment or facilities you will need (e.g. a video recorder, tape recorder, slide projector and screen, a room which can be darkened for showing slides). Check the room and equipment beforehand.

An example of an artist giving an introductory talk is given on page 74.

Checklist:
a project planning guide

You may wish to consider these points in planning your project.

✔ There is a project coordinator.

✔ There is a project plan which has been agreed by artist and teachers.

✔ The plan covers:

- aims, objectives and success criteria

- which pupils will take part

- structure, content and timing

- who is responsible for what

- materials and equipment

- proposed evaluation.

✔ The school and artist have formalised their agreement by signing a written contract.

✔ Pupils have been selected and informed about the project.

✔ The whole school has been made aware of the artist's visit.

✔ Materials and equipment have been ordered/obtained.

✔ The content of the first few sessions has been planned in some detail.

✔ Rooms are booked and the workspace has been prepared.

✔ The artist has prepared for working with pupils.

This short chapter contains the following elements:

- making introductions
- monitoring progress
- sharing the project
- consolidation and development.

What happens during the project itself depends on the type and purpose of the involvement. Many decisions will have been made at the planning stage which will shape the project as it progresses. This chapter is addressed to artists and teachers involved in a longer-term placement or residency, but those involved in shorter initiatives should also find the principles outlined here of interest.

Making introductions

The school community may already have been alerted to the project through a display and/or information sheet. The first step when the project actually begins is for the project coordinator to make sure that key members of staff know the artist is in school.

- The project coordinator should be on hand to welcome the artist and show him or her around the school.

- If the artist has not met all the members of staff involved in the project, this should be arranged as soon as possible.

- The artist should meet the headteacher (if he or she hasn't already done so).

- Introductions to other key members of staff, such as the school secretary, bursar and caretaker should be arranged.

Introducing pupils to the project

Pupils may find it difficult to understand what it means to be a professional artist. If this understanding is lacking, the project will not achieve its full potential. Talking about the artist's professional background at the beginning of a residency enables the pupils and staff to understand the artistic and commercial environment in which the artist operates. It brings home the 'special' nature of the project, and provides a foundation upon which teachers and pupils can build a relationship with the artist as a professional.

One means of establishing this context is for pupils to visit the artist's place of work (theatre, studio, gallery, etc.). This not only helps pupils to get to know the artist; it could form an important part of their developing understanding of the arts world. Another strategy is for the artist to give an introductory talk.

Case study

At the beginning of a weaver's residency, a meeting was held for him to discuss his work with a group of Year 10 students . The weaver talked about himself and his work, stressing the process of designing and making. He showed the students examples of his sketchbooks, 'my books of dreams', which he used to record his ideas. He explained that when he wanted to work up an idea, he made a larger paper design, from which he could weave a sample. He had brought some small samples of weaving with him which he encouraged the students to examine: 'The bits of material I've handed round are there so you can touch them; they're all woven sketches,' he explained.

The weaver showed the students a selection of slides, giving a brief history of tapestry, from Egyptian and medieval examples to the present day. He showed slides of himself at work in his studio and examples of his work, together with source material, sketches, designs and collages. (Later in the residency, he brought in some examples of his finished work for the pupils to discuss.)

This introductory meeting established a positive beginning to the residency. When the weaver explained about the history of tapestry and demonstrated his design process, the students became absorbed and motivated to try weaving for themselves. As one girl explained: 'Rather than just sticking this tapestry in front of you, you could actually see how he built up his designs. I thought he just got it out of his head and started weaving, but he didn't.' A boy added: 'I was a bit ignorant, I think, I didn't really care about things like weaving ... he [the weaver] started handing pieces of work round and that's when I got interested.'

The artist's talk and demonstration should create an atmosphere of excitement and a real sense that the project has begun at last. However, some artists feel quite intimidated at being asked to demonstrate and discuss their work in front of a large group. This is where negotiation between artists and teachers is important — perhaps a teacher could take on the role of introducing the artist to the pupils.

Monitoring progress

Artists and teachers should find the time to review the progress of the project as it is taking place. Brief informal discussions should take place at the end of each session/day. Ideally, there will be enough in the project budget to enable more formal discussion meetings to be held at regular intervals, to monitor progress in relation to the project plan. Notes of the points covered and the actions agreed should be circulated to all concerned.

Use the project plan and timetable as a basis for discussion, together with information gained from evaluation of progress (including feedback from pupils). Discussion could focus on three main areas: the allocation of responsibilities; reactions to the project; and progress to date.

Allocation of responsibilities

Topics for discussion at a review meeting might centre on the following questions.

- How is the planned allocation of responsibilities between artist and teachers working out in practice?

- Are artist and teachers happy with the responsibilities they have taken on?

Changes in responsibility which are already taking place should be acknowledged and discussed, as happened in the following example.

Case study

An artist was working with a GCSE art class where several small groups of students were producing lino prints. They had already produced some initial sketches and had reached the stage of transferring their designs onto pieces of lino. The artist circulated among groups of students who were about to begin work, while the teacher helped other groups with their designs. It became apparent to the teacher that the students all needed the same guidance from the artist at this stage, so they could mark out their designs on the lino and use the appropriate tools to begin cutting. The teacher pointed this out to the artist, and asked him if he would mind talking to the whole class at once. With his agreement, she called the class together and asked him to explain the necessary techniques. She helped by asking him questions, and checking that the students had understood what to do next.

When they later discussed this, the artist admitted that he did not feel at ease talking to large groups, but would be willing to do so when the teacher felt it was appropriate, as long as she was on hand to provide support. They agreed to adopt this strategy in future.

Reactions to the project

Topics for discussion might include:

- the level of pupil participation in, and engagement with, the project

- teachers' participation and interest

- the artist's participation and interest

- relationships between artist and teachers

- relationships between artist and pupils.

It is important to monitor pupils' participation and interest in the project. It could be that some groups of pupils seem to be taking a more active part than others — is it possible to identify any patterns which may explain the reactions of different groups? How can certain groups/individuals be encouraged to take a more active role?

If some members of staff, pupils (or even the artist) seem to be losing interest and direction, it is vital to find out why this is happening and to ask what they feel can be done to put the situation right. If a serious problem begins to affect the relationship between the artist and members of staff, it is important to sort it out quickly and not allow it to go unresolved. This is where the coordinator can act as a mediator, talking to both sides in order to get to the bottom of the problem. If the difficulty lies between the artist and the project coordinator, then it could be useful for both to have access to another source of support such as the headteacher, an external coordinator, or an LEA adviser/ inspector.

Progress

Topics for discussion include:

- progress in achieving the project's aims and objectives

- assessing pupil progress

- progress in relation to the timetable.

Aims and objectives

The project's aims, objectives and success criteria will form a useful framework for judging progress. Look at the original aims and decide how well each of them is being achieved. Use the success criteria as indicators of the progress of the project to date.

Keep a critical stance towards the aims and objectives themselves, remaining flexible enough to allow for exciting developments without losing sight of the original purpose of the project. You may find it helpful to consider the following questions.

● Are the original aims, objectives and success criteria still appropriate to the project?

● Do any of them need to be changed?

● Are there new areas emerging from the project that could usefully be added?

● Are there any aims in the original plan that have become less relevant and could be dropped?

● What would be the consequences if our original plans were changed at this stage of the project?

Pupil progress

It is important to discuss pupil progress. Observations of pupils' work, together with information from the evaluation process, will inform your discussion. You may find it helpful to focus on whether pupils are acquiring the necessary skills and concepts; and the quality of their work to date.

A related issue is the pacing of the project — are new skills and concepts being introduced at the right pace, or is the pace either too slow (causing loss of impetus) or too fast (causing lack of understanding and failure to master the basics)? It may be relevant to discuss whether an appropriate balance is being struck between process and product.

Timetable

Use the project timetable to assess whether the project is roughly on target. One of the problems encountered during residencies is that of judging, in advance, the amount of time that will be needed. Usually the problem is one of shortage of time — the progress is simply slower than was originally hoped. Keeping an eye on progress is important, especially since it allows for action to be taken (e.g. by arranging for extra, lunchtime sessions for the pupils to 'catch up') before time runs out.

Sharing the project

There are many ways of sharing the project with others, and this can be done while it is in progress, as well as when the work is completed.

Opportunities for teachers

Artists-in-schools projects can provide opportunities for teachers not already participating in the project to get involved; for example you could hold 'open sessions', workshops or training courses. This is a good means of raising awareness of the project among the school staff and spreading the impact of the artist's presence in a school. However, these events require their own planning and preparatory work, and artists must be paid adequately for taking on an INSET role.

Visitors

One means of sharing the project with the rest of the school is to invite small groups of pupils and teachers to visit. Others, such as governors, LEA advisers/inspectors, local authority arts officers, education officers from arts organisations, and sponsors may wish to visit the project at some time.

As we suggested in Chapter 1, it is a good idea to work out a strategy for dealing with visitors. You could consider:

- limiting the number of visitors per day

- appointing a pupil to guide visitors round and answer questions

- providing information about the project for visitors, such as an information sheet or display.

Displays and bulletins

A good method of keeping others informed is to maintain a display of work at a central point within the school. Such a display may already have been set up before the artist's arrival: this could be regularly updated (e.g. by including photographs of activities and samples of work).

Updating a display can be time-consuming for the teacher or artist to manage alone: this is where pupils can usefully be involved (e.g. in collecting, selecting and displaying the work). A display helps to keep everyone in touch with the work of the project and benefits pupils by involving them in presenting their work in progress to an audience. In the following example, the school set up a reporters' group to keep everyone informed about their project.

Case study

A secondary school decided to involve pupils in reporting on an arts week. The project involved Year 8 students and teachers working with a number of artists on a cross-curricular theme. A small group of Year 9 students were given the task of reporting on the project, with guidance from an English teacher. They set to work by interviewing artists, teachers and pupils, observing workshops and photographing events. The reporters put together a 'wall paper' — a display of word-processed articles and photographs, which changed daily. Students gathered by the display each morning, eagerly awaiting news. The wall paper became the chief information exchange among the participants, and between the participants and others in the school.

This reporters' group was a very positive aspect of the project and fulfilled three main functions. First, it informed the school of the progress of the work. Second, it enabled the students to explore aspects of media education. Third, the information collected was used as a record of the project, which fed into an evaluation of the work as it took place.

A final event

Many residencies involve working towards a final display or performance for the school, parents and sometimes for a wider audience. Putting on such an event requires planning: some schools may wish to involve students in various aspects of running this part of a project. When planning a final event it might be helpful to address the following questions.

Type of event

- What is the purpose of the event?

- What type of event will it be (e.g. performance, exhibition, screening, or a combination of these)?

- How will the artist's contribution to the project be demonstrated (for example, by including examples of the artist's work; having the artist perform alongside pupils; or by the artist introducing the work)?

- Will it be possible to show/explain some of the processes which have led up to this event?

Audience

- Who will the audience be (teachers and pupils within the school, parents, governors, community groups, other schools)?

- If appropriate, how will people from outside the school be encouraged to attend (e.g. through publicity material, which pupils could design and distribute)?

- Would it be appropriate to seek coverage in the local press?

Venue

- What kind of space is required?

- What equipment/resources are needed (e.g. sprung floor; film projector, screen and blackout facilities)?

- What other facilities are required (e.g. dressing rooms)?

- Should the event take place at the school or at another venue?

- If at another venue:

  how will pupils be involved (e.g. selling tickets, showing people round)?

  will venue staff be involved/on hand to assist?

  how much will it cost? (e.g. what proportion of the takings will the school receive)?

Consolidation and development

All that remains is to evaluate the impact of the project as a basis for consolidation and development. This could involve holding a feedback meeting for school staff and artists. The purpose of the meeting would be to review the success of the project so that artists and teachers are able to build on the outcomes to develop their work in the future (see Chapter 6 page 85).

Artists will want to consider what they have learned from this project as a basis for planning their next involvement with schools. Most teachers will have a fairly clear idea of whether and how they want to follow up the project with the pupils who took part. They may also wish to consider how the project could benefit other pupils in the future through teacher and/or curriculum development initiatives. An evaluation report will help to identify the positive outcomes of the project and to provide a good starting point for discussion about how to use the project as a stimulus for further work.

Evaluating the project is discussed in more detail in the following chapter.

Checklist:
the project in action

You may wish to check that the following actions are taking place during the project.

At the beginning

- ✔ The artist is introduced to key members of staff.
- ✔ The artist's professional context is demonstrated through a visit to their working environment, a display about the artist and/or an introductory session for the pupils involved.

During the project

- ✔ Artist and teachers are working in partnership with one another.
- ✔ Time has been set aside for reviewing progress and agreeing changes of plan.
- ✔ Evaluation is taking place.
- ✔ A strategy has been adopted to keep others informed, and to deal with visitors.
- ✔ A final event has been organised.
- ✔ A feedback meeting has been arranged.

Afterwards

- ✔ The outcomes of the project have been evaluated.
- ✔ Artists and teachers have considered their plans for further development in the light of messages from the project evaluation.

evaluation 6

In this chapter, we explain why evaluation is important and demonstrate what is involved in evaluating artists-in-schools work. The chapter provides an outline evaluation plan, together with guidance on time-efficient ways of collecting, interpreting and presenting information.

The main sections are as follows.

- What do we mean by evaluation?

- Why evaluate artists-in-schools work?

- An evaluation plan.

- Some questions to ask about your project.

- Collecting information.

- Holding a feedback meeting.

- Your evaluation report.

- What to do with the evaluation

- Sample response sheets.

What do we mean by evaluation?

Evaluation is the process of making evidence-based judgements about the value of a project. Although it recognises the significance of intuitive perceptions, the core of good evaluation is the collection of information from all groups of participants at key stages of the project. Evaluation builds on the process of monitoring (which is concerned with the progress of the project as it takes place) to look at the impact of the work in the short and longer term.

There are two main types of evaluation: formative and summative.

- Formative evaluation is primarily for the participants: it helps them to monitor progress and contributes to decision-making during the project.

- Summative evaluation provides a 'summing up' of the project after it has taken place, together with a judgement of its value and impact. As well as being useful for the participants, a summative evaluation report may be of interest to a wider audience (e.g. governors, funders, other artists and teachers).

Why evaluate artists-in-schools work?

Evaluation is important because artists-in-schools projects take funding, time and effort: resources which could have been used for other purposes. Those involved have a responsibility to account for their use of resources. Hard evidence of the educational and artistic value of an artists-in-schools project will help raise the status of this type of work in the school, and evaluation findings can be used to make the case for funding for more opportunities like this in the future.

Self-evaluation by artists and teachers provides opportunities for reflection, contributes to the development of their own professional practice and provides them with a better understanding of what they can contribute to this kind of work. Evaluation findings will also provide a basis on which to plan for future projects.

If artists-in-schools work is to develop and mature, then schools and artists, funders and researchers need documentation from projects which have taken place, and evidence of what does and doesn't work. In this way, they can learn from the experience of others and help to improve practice in the artists-in-schools field.

An evaluation plan

Those involved in a project generally do not have the time to undertake a complex evaluation process. We have therefore chosen to focus on evaluation methods which are relatively straightforward and easy to use. We outline a structure which should ensure that evaluation links in with activities which are already taking place.

You may find it helpful to consider the following points when planning your evaluation.

- Clarify what (and who) the evaluation is for.
- Identify someone to take responsibility for the evaluation.
- Decide when to evaluate.
- Document progress.
- Find out how the participants are reacting during the project.
- Analyse results and identify areas for development.
- Report your findings.

Some questions to ask about your project

During your evaluation you may find it helpful to consider particular aspects of the project and to collect information to help you address the following questions.

The project's aims and objectives

- How ambitious was the project?
- Were the aims appropriate?
- Did the project fulfil its aims? (Check against success criteria.)
- Were the activities the most appropriate to enable the aims and objectives to be met?

Structure and organisation

- Was the project well structured?
- Was the time used effectively (e.g. was there sufficient time for planning)?
- Were the resources appropriate (e.g. workspace, materials)?
- Was the project well managed?

Quality of the teachers' and artist's contribution

- Did the artist demonstrate a good knowledge of the subject-matter?
- Were the activities appropriate to the age and ability of the pupils (did they enable all pupils to respond)?
- Was it clear to pupils what was expected of them (e.g. commitment, behaviour, quality of work)?
- Was the learning managed effectively (e.g. did teachers and artist ask questions which deepened pupils' knowledge and checked their understanding)?

Quality of pupils' responses

- Did the pupils enjoy what they were asked to do?
- Did they maintain concentration?
- Did pupils try to achieve their best standard?
- Did pupils show initiative and take responsibility for their work?

Roles and relationships

- Did pupils work well together and support one another?
- Did they work well with the artist and teachers?
- Were teachers and artist supportive of one another?
- Did the artist and teachers demonstrate a clear understanding of each other's role?

Quality of the work

- How did pupils' work compare with what they have achieved in the past?
- How did their work compare with the standard you might expect from pupils of this age and ability?
- Did their work demonstrate that they had understood and applied what they learned during the project?
- Did their work show originality?
- What was the standard achieved?

The outcomes

- What did the project achieve and for whom?
- What was its impact (what difference did it make)?
- Were there any unanticipated outcomes?

Areas for development

- What would we do differently next time?
- What have we learned from this project that we would like to put into practice?
- How might we achieve this?

Collecting information

You should try to represent the views of all key groups of participants. Here are some suggestions for making the process of collecting information more manageable.

Documents and visual records

- Make a file of project documents that can be used in the evaluation. This could consist of letters, notes of conversations and decisions agreed during planning/review meetings, as well as key project documents (e.g. project brief, budget, contract).

- Take photographs and/or video footage of the work in progress. (Make a note of when these were taken: i.e. at what stage of the project.)

- If appropriate, keep samples of the pupils' work.

You could consider involving pupils in collecting information, under guidance from a teacher. Their role could be to document the project, for example through photographs/video, and to conduct interviews or discussions with participants.

See the case study example of a 'reporters' group' on page 77.

Essays and journals

Many secondary syllabuses (e.g. GCSE, GNVQ and A-level) require students to develop skills of self-evaluation. Pupils' evaluations of their own progress can be a good basis for statements in their Records of Achievement.

- Ask pupils to write an essay describing what they liked most and what they liked least about the project, and why.

- For older students and longer residencies it may be appropriate for pupils to keep a journal noting their involvement in the project and their thoughts and feelings as the work takes place.

Response sheets

Essentially a short questionnaire, response sheets are familiar to many teachers and artists as a means of evaluating workshops and training courses. They are useful for evaluating specific events and may be used to sum up impressions at the end of a project. Because they are relatively quick to fill in and easy to analyse, response sheets are a suitable method for collecting information from a large number of people.

Sample response sheets for pupils, teachers and artists can be found on pages 89 – 95.

Interviews

Interviews are particularly useful for learning about participants' thoughts and feelings. Unlike response sheets, interviews enable you to clarify people's responses on the spot and to explore issues you may not have considered beforehand. However, because they are quite time-consuming, interviews are not often used as a method of evaluation, unless the school has appointed an external evaluator.

- If you do wish to use interviewing, you should identify a few key people (e.g. artist, project coordinator, head of department) and set aside some time to talk to them about the project.

- Prepare a set of questions to ask.

- Decide how to record the interview (e.g. written notes, tape recorder).

Observation

Observation can be a useful means of checking on progress and seeing how participants are reacting during the project. Finding time to observe sessions can be problematic, so it is probably best to view this as a back-up, rather than as a main method of collecting information. As an alternative, video could be used to provide a record of some of the sessions.

A feedback meeting

A feedback meeting is an effective means of getting people to focus on evaluation. Holding a feedback meeting at the end of a project is a useful way of promoting reflection about what the project has achieved and can lead into a discussion of what to do next.

You could use the list of questions on page 83 as a basis for your discussion.

- Plan the meeting well in advance so that everyone (including artists) will be able to attend.

- Decide who to invite. For example, should governors, parents or members of the funding body be invited?

- Decide who will chair the meeting and agree beginning and end times.

- Begin by stating that the purpose of the meeting is to find out what people thought about the project and to identify areas for development.

- Someone should make a note of the strengths, weaknesses (or areas for development) and action points, to provide a written record of the meeting for all concerned.

Case study

The staff at an infant school met to discuss their project, which had a focus on the visual arts but had also included short visits from a dancer and two musicians. The whole school participated in the project throughout the Autumn term. The teachers identified the following strengths and weaknesses of their project.

Strengths

1. Greeted enthusiastically by parents who commented on pupils' work which had been shown at a parents' evening.

2. Teachers and visiting artists gave pupils experiences of different music, stories and dance.

Weaknesses

1. Wrong term

   a) New intake of children and no time to find out about them.

   b) There was lots of arts/crafts work. Possible over emphasis on this aspect of the curriculum this term.

2. Not enough time to make the most of the visiting artists. Follow-up work was rushed.

The teachers involved in this project had begun to feel quite negative about it as it took place, because of competing demands being made on them at a particularly busy time of year. This review meeting provided staff with the opportunity to step back from their experience and to identify the positive as well as the negative aspects of their experiences. Although they did not go on to identify action points, there are some clear implications for any future project, concerning the timing of the project, the amount of time allocated to the different art-form areas, and the use of the artists' visits.

Your evaluation report

You do not have to present the results of the evaluation in a written report, although you will probably need to produce something in writing at some stage. Funders may require you to submit a written report which can be reproduced and circulated to interested parties.

In any evaluation report, it is important to distinguish between the following three aspects:

- an account of what happened (fact)

- the views of participants about what happened (opinion)

- your analysis of this information (evaluation).

Analysing information

You will need to analyse your information before you can produce an evaluation report. Start by sorting out your material: make notes of where to find information about each of the areas of interest (e.g. there may be information on the quality of pupils' work from project documents, as well as in pupil response sheets).

The next step is to investigate the information you have collected. Your approach will differ according to the type of information you have collected (i.e. quantitative or qualitative).

Quantitative information

This is information which can be easily counted. It includes factual records, such as the number of sessions and pupils involved; and replies to 'closed' questions in interviews and on response sheets (e.g. yes/no responses and rating scales).

Make a record of any straightforward information, such as the number of sessions, and summarise answers to yes/no questions. Taking one question at a time, record the number of respondents who answered yes, no and those who did not respond. You may wish to add up the responses from a group of individuals (e.g. teachers or pupils).

Rating scales require a little more work to analyse. The simplest method is to count the number of people who answered Strongly Agree, Agree, etc. This will give you a good idea of the range of answers in relation to the number of people who responded.

Qualitative information

This is information which is more difficult to quantify. It includes opinions, views, thoughts, feelings and observations which may have come from a variety of sources (e.g. documents, answers to open-ended questions in response sheets, and pupils' journals/essays).

Start by reading through all the material relating to the same issue (e.g. everyone's answers to the same/similar questions). The aim is to group 'like' answers together into a number of categories. You may have to experiment with the headings until you find a grouping that fits the majority of answers.

For example, you could end up by grouping all the answers to the question 'What did you like most about this project?' into six categories:

1 opportunities for new learning

2 meeting a professional artist

3 the artist's personal qualities (enthusiasm, ability to motivate pupils)

4 the opportunity for a group of pupils and teachers to work together

5 the final event

6 other benefits (e.g. involvement of parents, use of new materials).

You can count the number of people in each group who gave a particular type of response and see how this relates to the total number of people who commented. As you look through your material, you could make a note of any quotes which illustrate a point made by several people, for use in your report.

When you have identified your main findings and are fairly sure you have established why these have occurred, you can consider how best to report the results of the evaluation.

Writing your report

A good report should be both descriptive and interpretative. It should help readers to understand what happened, what those involved thought about the project and the impact of the project in the school. It should be logically structured, clearly written and not too long. An outline structure for an evaluation report is given below.

Section 1

- Acknowledgements (e.g. thanks to the project sponsors).

- Introduction and background to the project, including a brief description of school, where the project idea originated, how it was funded and who took part.

- Aims of the project and its structure.

- A short description of the project itself (what happened).

- An outline of the approach to evaluation (e.g. methods and contributors).

Section 2

- Evaluation findings.

- Conclusions.

- Future developments.

Your report could include examples of work, photographs, etc., but remember that the primary purpose of the report is to present the findings of the evaluation, not to tell the story of the project. Section 2 will make up the bulk of the report and is discussed in more detail below.

Evaluation findings

Begin by reporting the points of greatest importance (e.g. the main project outcomes). Your readers will be interested in the reactions of the participants (pupils, teachers, artists) to the different elements of the project. Explain whether most people were in agreement, then highlight where there was a difference of opinion or reaction and discuss why.

Help other people to understand the importance of your points. For example, a statement that 'very few pupils dropped out of the project' becomes more significant if you explain that (a) only two out of 65 pupils withdrew; (b) pupils were free to leave the project at any time; and (c) the project attracted and retained several pupils who had a previously poor record of school attendance.

It is a good idea to use specific examples and quotes to illustrate people's reactions, but try to avoid reproducing long extracts from response sheets or interview transcripts. If you do use quotes, make it clear whether or not they are representative of a commonly held view.

Conclusion and future developments

Try to reach a conclusion about each aspect of the project, drawing together the key points you have made in your discussion of the findings (e.g. main strengths and weaknesses/areas for development). You could also write a concluding statement about the success of the project and its overall impact on the school.

Use the results of the evaluation to make suggestions about future work in the school. You could also talk about how the project's impact on the school might affect development in certain areas (for example, INSET or the school's arts policy) in the context of the school development plan.

Negotiating final content

Once you have written the report, you should check it for factual errors and to ensure that you have respected confidentiality where this has been promised. If possible, circulate a draft to the teachers and artist(s) involved. Ask them to check for any factual inaccuracies and that you have not missed any key points or misinterpreted the information.

If someone disagrees with something you have written, it does not necessarily mean that you should remove it from your report. If you are sure that you have reported the evidence correctly, and believe the point to be an important one, then you should explain this to the person. You may be able to negotiate a different way of making the point which is acceptable to both of you, or you could agree to add a note in the report that not everyone was in agreement with your interpretation.

What to do with the evaluation

The evaluation can have two main functions: self-evaluation for participating artists and teachers; and informing others.

Self-evaluation for artists and teachers involved

The report will provide a useful means of self-evaluation for the professionals who took part. They will be able to compare their assessment of how they contributed to the project with that of their colleagues and the pupils. The report should also provide a means for the school to assess the contribution of the project as a whole to its own performance in specific curriculum areas. It will help to identify what worked well and areas in need of development. This can provide a useful basis for artists and teachers to consider how to capitalise on strengths and address any areas of weakness when planning future artists-in-schools projects.

Informing others about the project

Decide who else you would like to read the report. The list will probably include school governors and any external funders. You could also consider sending the report to the relevant LEA adviser(s), your RAB or National Arts Council and anyone else who is likely to have a particular interest in the project. If the report has provided evidence of the benefits of this project and has identified areas for further work, you are in a good position to use it to help argue the case for more resources from heads, governors and other funders.

Sample response sheets

We have included three examples of response sheets, which could be used to gather information from pupils, artists and teachers. The examples include two types of questions. Closed questions (yes/no or 'tick a box') are quick to fill in and it is relatively easy to quantify the answers. Open-ended questions ('What do you think about...?') are useful for gathering qualitative information, such as feelings and opinions, but they take longer to analyse.

We have chosen a specific example to illustrate how response sheets could be designed. In this case,

Year 6 pupils from St James' Middle School have attended a concert of Stravinsky's *Rite of Spring* by the Framworth Orchestra, and some of the musicians have visited the school to work with pupils on a related composition. There are three response sheets, designed for pupils, teachers and musicians.

Although this was a short-term involvement, the response sheets could be adapted for use in a longer-term project. For example, you could ask participants to fill in a short questionnaire at the beginning of a residency, giving an insight into their preparation for and expectations of a project; and again at the end of the project, asking for their reflections on the implementation and impact of the work.

Designing a response sheet

When designing response sheets, it may be helpful to consider the following points.

1. Pupils are more likely to give full responses if they do not have to give their names. But you may need some background information to help you interpret pupils' reactions. In this example, it is anticipated that pupils who are learning to play an instrument may react differently from those who are not, so this information is requested on the response sheet.

2. Rating scales are a useful way of getting a general impression of people's reactions. The statements need to be short, simple and unambiguous. Try to include both positive and negative statements. Three-point scales are appropriate for younger pupils (represented by faces in this example), but you may wish to use four- or five-point scales for older pupils and adults, because they are able to provide a more detailed impression of people's views.

Pupil response sheet

We would like to find out what you thought about working with the players from the Framworth Orchestra. This will help us to plan other activities in future. Please spare a few minutes to give us your views. You need not give your name.

1. Are you learning to play an instrument? (*Please tick*)   Yes ⬭   No ⬭

   If you ticked *Yes*, please tell us which instrument(s) you play

2. Please tick one face in each line to show what you thought about the musicians' visit.

   ☺ = **I agree** with this

   😐 = **I don't know** what I think about this

   ☹ = **I do not agree** with this

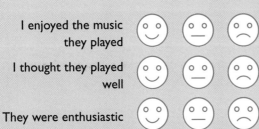

Here is an example   I like doing lots of homework   ☺ 😐 ☹✓

About the pre-concert talk

The talk was interesting   ☺ 😐 ☹

It helped me appreciate the music   ☺ 😐 ☹

I would have liked some more information   ☺ 😐 ☹

About the concert

I enjoyed the music they played   ☺ 😐 ☹

I thought they played well   ☺ 😐 ☹

They were enthusiastic   ☺ 😐 ☹

It went on too long   ☺ 😐 ☹

About the group work

I liked working with the musicians   ☺ 😐 ☹

I found out what it is like to play in an orchestra   ☺ 😐 ☹

I learned a lot about Russian music   ☺ 😐 ☹

They explained clearly what we were supposed to do   ☺ 😐 ☹

I found it hard to concentrate   ☺ 😐 ☹

We could try our own ideas   ☺ 😐 ☹

It was too difficult   ☺ 😐 ☹

There wasn't enough time   ☺ 😐 ☹

General impressions

I enjoyed this project

I found it interesting

It was a good way to learn

I would like to do something like this again

3. What did you like **most** about the musicians' visit to the school? (Please explain why.)

4. What did you like **least** about their visit? (Please explain why.)

5. If we were planning to do this again, is there anything you think we should change?

6. Do you have any other comments on this project or on what you would like us to arrange in future?

Thank you for answering these questions and telling us what you thought about this visit. Please return your completed sheet to Mrs James.

Teacher response sheet

We would like to find out what you thought about our involvement with the players from the Framworth Orchestra. This will contribute to our evaluation report and help us in planning new developments. Please spare a few minutes to give us your views. You need not give your name.

1. This project had three main aims. Please indicate how far you think each of these was realised by circling a number and adding a brief comment.

   a) To enable pupils to respond to and evaluate a high-quality live music performance.

   Not at all   Fully achieved

   | 1 | 2 | 3 | 4 | 5 |

   Comment:

   b) To help pupils to develop an understanding of twentieth-century Russian music.

   Not at all   Fully achieved

   | 1 | 2 | 3 | 4 | 5 |

   Comment:

   c) To produce a group composition, taking Stravinsky's *Rite of Spring* as a starting point.

   Not at all   Fully achieved

   | 1 | 2 | 3 | 4 | 5 |

   Comment:

2. a) How were you involved in the musicians' visit to the school?

   b) Would you have preferred a different role? (Please explain.)

3. What did your pupils learn from the experience as a whole?

4.   a) What did you like **most** about the musicians' input?

        b) What did you like **least** about the musicians' input?

5. Is there anything you would suggest the musicians change next time they visit a school?

6. Do you plan to follow up this project in any way? (Please explain.)

7. Do you have any other comments on the project or suggestions about what you would like the school to arrange in future?

Thank you very much for giving your time to answer these questions.
Please return your completed sheet to Mrs James by 30th January.

evaluation

Artist response sheet

We would like to find out what you thought about your involvement with St James' Middle School. This will contribute to our evaluation report and help us in planning new developments. Please spare a few minutes to give us your views.

1. Please circle one number in each row to show your level of agreement with each of the following statements (5 = Strongly Agree; 4 = Agree; 3 = Neutral; 2 = Disagree; 1 = Strongly Disagree).

The school provided sufficient information to help us plan the visit	5	4	3	2	1
We felt welcome in the school	5	4	3	2	1
The pupils spoke enthusiastically about the concert	5	4	3	2	1
The pupils were well prepared	5	4	3	2	1
The pupils were well behaved	5	4	3	2	1
There wasn't enough time	5	4	3	2	1
The teachers supported our work in the classroom	5	4	3	2	1
The pupils worked well in groups	5	4	3	2	1
Too many pupils were involved in the group work	5	4	3	2	1

2. What do you feel the pupils gained from
   a) the concert?

   b) your visit to the school?

3. Please comment on the teachers' involvement with your work.

4. If we were planning a similar project in future, is there anything you would suggest we change?

5. Do you have any other comments about the visit?

Thank you very much for giving your time to answer these questions.
Please return your completed sheet to Mrs James by 30th January.

Checklist: evaluation

The actions you might like to take in evaluating your project include the following:

✔ clarify what (and who) the evaluation is for

✔ identify someone to take responsibility for the evaluation

✔ decide when to evaluate

✔ find an appropriate means of documenting what happens (e.g. through video, photographs and/or project documents)

✔ find out how artist, teachers and pupils are reacting during the project by using essays and journals, response sheets, interviews and/or observation

✔ hold a feedback meeting

✔ analyse evaluation results and identify areas for development

✔ report your findings

✔ decide how to capitalise on what has been learned from the evaluation of this project in planning what to do next.

resources:
contacts and further reading

This chapter contains:

- information on national, regional and local contacts
- a comprehensive listing of relevant publications.

National and regional contacts

We have listed the national and regional organisations that offer guidance, advice (and in some cases funding) to those involved in artists-in-schools work.

The Arts Council of England

14 Great Peter Street
London SW1P 3NQ
Tel: 0171 333 0100

The Education and Training Department at ACE works at a strategic level, providing a national lead on arts education and training. It helps to bring together arts and education professionals through establishing network groups, some of which include artists. Each of the art-form departments has an education specialist. ACE produces a number of publications on work in education, some of which are listed below. Although ACE departments occasionally run artists-in-education schemes, information about and funding for artists-in-schools work are generally best obtained from the relevant Regional Arts Board.

The Arts Council of Wales

9 Museum Place
Cardiff CF1 3NX
Tel: 01222 394711

The Arts Council of Wales supports artists-in-schools activity through grant-aid for specialist arts organisations, such as the national network of theatre-in-education companies and community arts organisations. It supports residency and community touring programmes, to which access by schools is encouraged. The Council has piloted artists-in-schools brokering projects and is undertaking, with other agencies in Wales, a policy review of arts and education activity.
Contact the Director of Policy and Planning for further details.

The Scottish Arts Council

12 Manor Place
Edinburgh EH3 7DD
Tel: 0131 226 6051

The Scottish Arts Council aims to encourage artists-in-schools work through the establishment of networks, and the promotion of artists-in-schools schemes. The Council has publications of interest to those involved in this area of work.
Contact the Senior Education Officer for further details.

The Arts Council of Northern Ireland

185 Stranmillis Road
Belfast BT9 5DU
Tel: 01232 381591

The Arts Council of Northern Ireland has some funding available for artists-in-schools projects and supports a programme of tours to primary schools. There is a directory of artists available for work in schools.
Contact the Education Officer for further details.

The British Film Institute

21 Stephen Street
London W1P 2LN
Tel: 0171 255 1444

The BFI publishes a variety of resources on media education, and occasionally contributes funding to school-based projects.
Contact the Principal Education Officer for further details.

The Crafts Council

44a Pentonville Road
Islington
London N1 9BY
Tel: 0171 278 7700

The Crafts Council distributes funds to the Regional Arts Boards in England and the Arts Council of Wales for allocation to crafts projects in their regions.

The Council holds two registers of crafts workers, some of whom are available for work in schools. The *Index of Selected Makers* comprises makers who have been selected for the quality and standard of their work. Images of their work and bibliographies are entered on to the *Photostore*, a computerised database which enables users to search for images and information. Visitors to the Council's London address can use the *Photostore* free of charge. Prints or slides of the images are available by post.

Contact the Council's Photostore and Reference Library for further details.

ABSA

Nutmeg House
60 Gainsford Street
Butlers Wharf
London SE1 2NY
Tel: 0171 378 8143

The Association for Business Sponsorship of the Arts (ABSA) encourages business sponsorship of the arts (see page 47). It has six offices covering: the South, Midlands, and North of England; Northern Ireland; Scotland; and Wales.

Contact ABSA for details of its *Pairing Scheme*.

National arts associations and networks

There are a number of arts associations and organisations which are involved in artists-in-schools work. These include: the National Association for Writers in Education, the Association of Professional Theatre for Children and Young People, the Community

Dance and Mime Foundation, *Engage* (the national association for gallery education) and *Sound Sense* (the community music association). There are also organisations specialising in arts and disability work, most of which belong to the National Disability Arts Forum or the National Network of Arts and Disability Agencies.

If you wish to contact these organisations, we suggest you use *The Education Yearbook* (see page 105) or ask the relevant officer at your National Arts Council/RAB for current contact details.

English Regional Arts Boards

There are ten Regional Arts Boards (RABs) in England, each of which is responsible for the funding and development of the arts in a particular region. The RABs work closely with the Arts Council of England, from which they receive most of their funding.

Whereas the national funding bodies take responsibility for arts development at a national level (for example, running nationally significant schemes, assessing applications for National Lottery funding for capital development projects and funding companies with a national remit), the RABs work at a regional level, providing advice, information, training and funding to the arts organisations and artists in their region. Policy development is collaborative, with ACE, the other national funding bodies and the RABs working together to ensure that the various organisations which make up the English funding system are working to the same agreed policy. Each RAB interprets policy according to the particular needs of its region.

Eastern Arts Board

Cherry Hinton Hall
Cherry Hinton Road
Cambridge CB1 4DW
Tel: 01223 215 355

Area covered: Bedfordshire, Cambridgeshire, Essex, Hertfordshire, Lincolnshire, Norfolk, Suffolk.

East Midlands Arts Board

Mountfields House
Epinal Way
Loughborough
Leics LE11 0QE
Tel: 01509 218 292

Area covered: Derbyshire, (excluding High Peak District), Leicestershire, Northamptonshire, Nottinghamshire.

London Arts Board

Elme House
133 Long Acre
Covent Garden
London WC2E 9AF
Tel: 0171 240 1313

Area covered: the London boroughs and the Corporation of the City of London.

Northern Arts Board

9–10 Osborne Terrace
Jesmond
Newcastle upon Tyne NE2 1NZ
Tel: 0191 281 6334

Area covered: Cumbria, Durham, Northumberland; unitary authorities of Hartlepool, Middlesbrough, Redcar and Cleveland, Stockton; metropolitan districts of Newcastle, Gateshead, North Tyneside, Sunderland and South Tyneside.

North West Arts Board

Manchester House
22 Bridge Street
Manchester M3 3AB
Tel: 0161 834 6644

Area covered: Cheshire, Lancashire, Merseyside, Greater Manchester and High Peak District of Derbyshire.

Southern Arts Board

13 St Clement Street
Winchester
Hants SO23 9DQ
Tel: 01962 855 099

Area covered: Berkshire, Buckinghamshire, Hampshire, Isle of Wight, Oxfordshire, Wiltshire, south east Dorset.

South East Arts Board

10 Mount Ephraim
Tunbridge Wells
Kent TN4 8AS
Tel: 01892 515 210

Area covered: Kent, Surrey, East Sussex, West Sussex.

South West Arts

Bradninch Place
Gandy Street
Exeter EX4 3LS
Tel: 01392 218 188

Area covered: Cornwall, Devon, Dorset (except districts of Bournemouth, Christchurch and Poole), Gloucestershire and Somerset; unitary authorities of Bristol, Bath and North East Somerset, South Gloucestershire, North Somerset.

West Midlands Arts

82 Granville Street
Birmingham B1 2LH
Tel: 0121 631 3121

Area covered: Hereford &
Worcester, Shropshire, Staffordshire, Warwickshire; metropolitan districts of Birmingham, Coventry, Dudley, Sandwell, Solihull, Walsall and Wolverhampton.

Yorkshire & Humberside Arts Board

21 Bond Street
Dewsbury
West Yorkshire WF13 1AX
Tel: 01924 455 555

Area covered: North Yorkshire; unitary authorities of York, Hull, East Riding, North Lincolnshire, North East Lincolnshire; metropolitan districts of Barnsley, Bradford, Calderdale, Doncaster, Kirklees, Leeds, Rotherham, Sheffield, Wakefield.

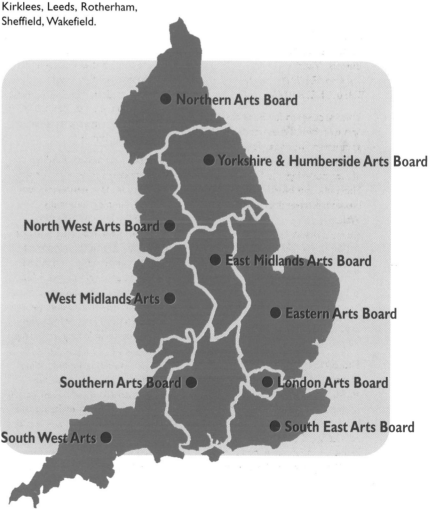

Local contacts

Whether you are looking for information, advice, funding or details of the artists-in-schools projects currently 'on offer' in your area, there are various local people you can contact. Most of these people operate mailing lists which you can join (often free of charge).

Local authority arts officers

Most local authorities employ arts officers who are responsible for developing policy and strategy for the arts in their area. Many place a particular emphasis on arts education work with people of all ages. Most officers initiate and fund various arts education projects, some of which are attached to professional arts events. Some officers hold databases of artists available for work in education.

Contact your arts officer via the local authority's central offices.

Animateurs and arts development workers

These posts are often jointly funded by local authorities and Regional Arts Boards. They are usually art-form specific (some areas have a number of workers specialising in different art forms). Education and/or participatory arts work is part of an animateur's brief. Animateurs and development workers are usually artists in their own right.

Contact your RAB or National Arts Council to find out if there are animateurs or development workers in your area.

Education officers in arts organisations

Many arts organisations (such as galleries, theatres, arts centres, art-house cinemas, and concert venues) have an education officer whose role is to develop education work linked to the artistic programme of the organisation. Education activities can range from school- or community-based residency projects and workshops, to pre-performance talks, gallery education days and weekend INSET sessions. Some organisations run an ongoing programme of activities which might include tours of the building, work experience and 'meet the artist' sessions. They may have a schools' membership scheme and produce an education newsletter.

Contact arts organisations in your area working in the relevant art form(s).

Arts education agencies

Arts education agencies are a relatively new idea, but their number is increasing. Some of the existing agencies are independent, while others operate from within an LEA service. However, they share the same function, which is to develop arts education activity in a particular geographical area, through initiating, managing and evaluating arts education projects. The key to their approach is the brokering of partnerships between funders, schools, LEAs, arts organisations, artists, and the wider community. The agencies have a major role in initiating artists-in-schools projects and are often the conduit for RAB and local authority funding for this type of work.

Contact your RAB or National Arts Council to find out if there is an agency operating in your area.

Relevant publications

Books on artists-in-schools projects for artists and teachers

The following publications are aimed at artists and teachers. They contain reports of initiatives and offer guidance on working together.

Close Collaborations: Art in Schools and the Wider Environment
Norman Binch and Sue Clive, Arts Council of England (1994). ISBN: 0 7287 0692 X.

Available from:
Trentham Books Ltd.
Westview House
734 London Road
Oakhill
Stoke-on-Trent ST4 5NP.

This book explores the use of museums, galleries, exhibitions, and professional artists as resources for teaching the visual arts in schools. The book begins with a short section highlighting issues and offering advice. This is followed by a number of case studies which provide examples of collaborative projects for pupils of different ages. It is illustrated with black and white photographs and contains a list of suggested further reading.

Live Art in Schools
Richard Layzell, Arts Council of England (1993). ISBN: 0 728 0671 7.

Available from:
Combined Arts Department
Arts Council of England.

This book uses examples of projects in schools to explain what live art is and how its practitioners can contribute to the work of schools. Illustrated with black and white photographs, the book contains suggestions on how live arts can be used to deliver aspects of the National Curriculum, and contains notes on how to organise a residency.

The Children's Music Book: Performing Musicians in Schools

Saville Kushner, Calouste Gulbenkian Foundation (1991).
ISBN: 0 903319 52 7.

Available from:
Turnaround Distribution Ltd.
27 Horsell Road
London N5 1XL.

This book is an account of the educational programme of the Birmingham City Orchestra's *Adopt-a-Player* Scheme. The book includes portrayals of the musicians' sessions with pupils in a number of schools; and extracts from interviews with pupils, teachers and players.

Under the Rainbow: Writers and Artists in Schools

David Morley, edited by Andy Mortimer, Northern Arts and Bloodaxe Books (1991).
ISBN: 1 85224 112 8.

Available from:
Bloodaxe Books Ltd
PO Box 1SN
Newcastle upon Tyne NE99 1SN.

This book arose from a Northern Arts conference where artists and teachers put forward their views on the philosophy and practicalities of artists-in-schools projects. The book offers advice on setting up and running projects in different art-form areas, drawing on examples of work in the region. It

is illustrated with black and white photographs, and has a listings section.

Artists in Wigan Schools

Rod Taylor, Calouste Gulbenkian Foundation (1991).
ISBN: 0 90331950 0.

Available from:
Turnaround Distribution Ltd.

In this book, Rod Taylor, Director of Wigan's Drumcroon Education Art Centre, describes the work of the artists-in-schools scheme he established. The scheme employed young artists in the year following their graduation from art and design courses. The artists set up studios in schools, dividing their time between their own work and working with pupils. The author presents case studies of a variety of projects, explaining what happened and the impact of the work on pupils, artists, teachers and the wider community. The book is extensively illustrated with colour photographs.

Please note: addresses are given in full the first time they appear.

Artists in Leeds Schools: a Review of Leeds City Council's Artists in Schools Programme

Dick Downing, Leeds City Council (1996).
ISBN: 0 9508029 2 1.

Available from:
Leeds City Council Department of Education
Advisory and Inspection Services
Floor 9 East
Merrion House
110 Merrion Centre
Leeds LS2 8DR.

Between 1991 and 1995, over half a million pounds was spent as a result of the Leeds Artists in Schools Programme, enabling more than 480 artists across a range of art forms to work in 335 schools. This book documents the results of the partnerships between artists and schools, and builds on their experiences to offer advice on planning, process, outcomes, and suggestions for developing the work. There is a series of case studies of artists-in-schools projects funded by the programme. The book is extensively illustrated with colour photographs and quotations from participating artists, teachers and pupils.

Learning Through Theatre: New Perspectives on Theatre in Education

Edited by Tony Jackson, Routledge (1993).
ISBN: 0 415 08610 8.

Available from:
Routledge
11 New Fetter Lane
London EC4P 4EE.

This book provides useful background reading for people with an interest in the development of theatre-in-education (TIE). It contains a series of essays addressing four main themes: the historical development of TIE in the UK; devising TIE programmes; international perspectives on TIE; and future directions. Several of the chapters are illustrated with extracts from scripts, and with black and white photographs of plays in performance.

Guide to Mime in Education

Jac Wilkinson, Mime Action Group (1994).
ISBN: 1 873142 02 1.

Available from:
Mime Action Group
The Circus Space
Coronet Street
London N1 6NU.

This book contains both a guide to the place of mime in the National Curriculum and case studies of mime artists working in schools, colleges and in the community. It is illustrated with black and white photographs throughout, and contains a listing of contact organisations and further reading.

Books on artists-in-schools projects for artists

The following publications contain guidance for artists wishing to work in educational settings.

Regular Marvels: a Handbook for Animateurs, Practitioners and Development Workers in Dance, Mime, Music and Literature

Edited by François Matarasso, CDMF (1994).
ISBN: 1 898409 01 3.

Available from:
Community Dance and Mime Foundation
13–15 Belvoir Street
Leicester LE1 6SL.

This book is aimed at dancers and mime artists working in the community. It contains sections on: residencies, workshops and classes; project planning; and funding. Although the text covers many different types of community work, there is some specific advice on working in schools. The book contains a series of chapters giving examples of community projects in dance, literature, mime, and music

— each written by an arts worker with experience in the field. There are sections listing further reading and contacts.

AN Publications publish a number of guides and resources for visual artists. The following publications are particularly helpful for artists wishing to work in education, and are available from:

AN Publications
PO Box 23
Sunderland SR4 6DG.

Art in Public: What, Why and How

Edited by Susan Jones, AN Publications (1992).
ISBN: 0 907730 18 3.

This is a guide for artists undertaking commissioned pieces of work in public spaces. The book contains information on approaches, working methods, presenting and developing the work. It is extensively illustrated with black and white photographs and contains a list of contacts.

Art with People

Edited by Malcolm Dickson, AN Publications (1995).
ISBN: 0 907730 23 X.

This book is about art as a socially-relevant practice, spanning the development of 'community arts' (i.e. artists working in the community) over the last 30 years. It contains a number of essays on the history of art as a vehicle for personal, social and community development; and has specific contributions on work in galleries, prisons and schools. The theory is backed up with case studies, many

written by artists who led the projects. The book is illustrated with black and white photographs from community-based projects, and has a useful contacts and further reading section.

Books on artists-in-schools projects for teachers

The following publications contain guidance for teachers wishing to work with professional artists.

Artists in Residence: a Teachers' Handbook

Sally Manser with Hannah Wilmot, London Arts Board and St. Katherine and Shadwell Trust (1995).
ISBN: 0 947784 25 X.

Available from:
London Arts Board.

This handbook offers practical advice to primary and secondary teachers on the different stages of a residency: from initiating a project and selecting an artist, through planning and preparation, to discussing the immediate and longer-term outcomes. It was originally commissioned by the St. Katherine and Shadwell Trust to support schools in Tower Hamlets in their work with artists in a variety of art-form areas. There are sections on relevant publications and sources of advice and funding (particularly relevant for schools in the London area). The book is illustrated with photo images and quotations from participants in artists-in-schools projects.

Arts Professionals in Schools: a Step by Step Guide to Artists-in-Schools Projects

Edited by Keith Winser, Norfolk Educational Press (1995).
ISBN 1 85526 201 0.

Available from:
Norfolk Inspection, Advice and Training Services
County INSET Centre
Witard Road
Norwich NR7 9XD.

This practical guide is aimed at teachers of arts subjects in secondary schools. It is based on the experiences of a number of schools working with artists in Cambridgeshire, Essex and Norfolk, as part of the Technical and Vocational Education Initiative (TVEI). It contains advice for teachers on each stage of a project, with particular emphasis on planning and evaluation as key elements of successful partnerships. The book is illustrated with examples drawn from work in schools, including quotations from participants, samples of students' work and photographs of projects in progress.

Now to Create: Arts and Education in Partnership

Sylvia Dow, Scottish Arts Council (1994).
ISBN: 1 85119 064 3.

Available from:
Scottish Arts Council.

This publication aims to help teachers to realise the full potential of the arts in education. It is in three parts: an overview of the arts in the curriculum in Scotland and the potential contribution of professional artists; a series of case studies describing projects in a

range of art forms; and a directory of Scottish organisations, artists and companies involved in this area of work. The book is illustrated with black and white photographs.

Dance Pack

Arts Council of England.
ISBN 0 7287 0702 0.

Available from:
Dance Department
Arts Council of England.

This pack is in two parts. *Dance Companies: How to Use Them* contains a booklet giving advice on working with dance companies and a listing of useful contacts, including dance company archives, museums and libraries, national dance agencies and organisations.

The second part of the pack provides a digest of educational resources offered by dance companies which are supported by revenue funding from a national or regional arts body. This comprises a series of factsheets written by each company, giving brief details of their artistic and education policy, tours, ways of working and resources; and contact details. The pack is updated regularly.

South Asian Dance in Schools: a Teacher's Handbook

Edited by Tessa Gordziejko, ADiTi (1995).

Available from ADiTi
Willowfield Street
Bradford BD7 2AH.

This handbook is designed for teachers wishing to work with professional South Asian dancers in a school environment. It provides guidance on the performance, choreography, and appreciation of South Asian dance. There are a number of examples of dance

activities linked to each of the four key stages of the National Curriculum, together with information on cultural context and guidance on working with a South Asian dancer. The book is illustrated with black and white photographs and has sections on further reading, videos and contact organisations.

Legal issues and safety

Visual Arts Contracts: Introduction
and
Visual Arts Contracts: Residencies

Nicholas Sharp,
AN Publications (1995).
Available from:
AN Publications.

Nicholas Sharp is a solicitor with experience of contracts in business and the arts. The first of these short publications gives general guidance on contracts, and the second provides a residency checklist, together with annotated sample contracts designed for residencies and workshops.

Protection of Children: Disclosure of Criminal Background of those with Access to Children (Circular 9/93)

Department for Education (1993).

Available from:
Teachers Branch
Department for Education and Employment
Corporation House
Staindrop Road
Darlington DL3 9BG.

This circular provides guidance for school governors and education authority officers on the arrangements for making criminal background checks on people employed to work with children. It clarifies the circumstances in which a background check may be warranted and lays out the procedure for doing so.

A Guide to Safe Practice in Art and Design

Department for Education (1995). ISBN: 0 11 270896 X.

Available from:
HMSO Publications Centre
PO Box 276
London SW8 5DT.

This comprehensive publication is aimed at teachers involved in art and design activities in schools. It contains information and guidance on: relevant legislation, safety education; management and organisation; accommodation; equipment and materials. There is also a section listing sources of further information. Although aimed primarily at a teacher audience, it would also prove useful reading for visual artists and crafts workers planning work in schools.

Evaluation

Partners No. 2: Evaluation. An Introduction to Evaluation for Artists Working in Schools

Phyllida Shaw, Arts Council of England (1991).

Available from:
Education and Training Department
Arts Council of England.

Intended for artists working in schools, this pack explains what evaluation is, and sets out how to approach evaluating an artists-in-schools project. It is a good basic introduction to evaluating this type

of work and would also be of use to teachers.

Funding and fundraising

There are numerous guides to funding and fundraising for education and the arts. We have selected the ones we think will be most useful for teachers and artists needing to raise money for artists-in-schools work.

Arts Funding System Pack

Arts Council of England (1995).

Available from:
Information Department — Library
Arts Council of England.

This loose-leaf pack comprises a series of factsheets on the arts funding system in the UK, including details of the remit and funding policy of the main organisations which administer public funding for the arts.

Fundraising: the Artist's Guide to Planning and Financing Work

Edited by Susan Jones, AN Publications (1993). ISBN: 0 907730 20 5.

Available from:
AN Publications.

This practical guide is aimed at helping visual artists to raise money for their work. There is advice on the main funding sources, devising a strategy and putting together proposals. The book includes a chapter on the do's and don'ts of making applications, drawing on the experience of people on the receiving end. There are numerous examples of successful projects and black and white photographs of funded work.

International Arts Quarterly Digest

Available from:
International Arts Bureau
Arts Council of England.

This bulletin gives updates on European funding programmes and lists contacts at ACE who can give you more detailed information on European grants.

Schools Funding Update

ISSN: 1360 7359.

Available from:
Pitman Publishing
128 Long Acre
London WC2E 9AN.

This monthly bulletin contains information on income-generation for schools, including articles on school fundraising and a digest of funding opportunities.

The Directory of Social Change publishes a number of fundraising guides, which are updated regularly. The ones listed below are particularly recommended.
These are available from:
Directory of Social Change Books
24 Stephenson Way
London NW1 2DP.

A Guide to the Major Trusts Volume 1

Luke Fitz Herbert, Susan Forrester and Julio Grau. ISBN 1 873860 49 8.

This guide provides detailed information about the 300 major trusts and foundations, including donations policies and contact details.

A Guide to the Major Trusts Volume 2

Paul Brown and David Casson.
ISBN 1 873860 64 1.

The second volume contains details of a further 700 trusts and foundations, together with a subject and geographical index to both volumes.

The Education Funding Guide: Support from Government, Trusts and Companies

Susan Forrester, Anne Mountfield and Alka Patel.
ISBN 1 873860 70 6.

This guide gives details of government funding and the major companies, trusts and foundations which support work in schools.

The Arts Funding Guide

Susan Forrester.
ISBN: 1 873860 97 8.

This guide covers sources of arts funding in the UK and Europe. There is advice on fundraising methods and information about the major funding sources, including the National Lottery.

Yearbooks

The following publications contain listings of relevant contacts and organisations, including contact details for LEA advisers, National Arts Council and RAB officers. They are updated each year. Both books are expensive, but your local library should be able to obtain a reference copy.

The Education Yearbook

Available from:
Pitman Publishing
128 Long Acre
London WC2E 9BR.

The Music Education Yearbook: the Guide for Parents, Teachers, Students and Musicians

Available from:
Rheingold Publications Ltd.
241 Shaftesbury Avenue
London WC2H 8EH.

Videos

We have listed two particularly useful videos showing artists working in schools.

Telling Tales

Directed by Patrick Redsell.

Available from:
Suffolk Inspection and Advice Division
Suffolk Education Department
St Andrew House
Ipswich IP4 1JL.

This video follows storyteller Hugh Lupton and puppeteer Mike McManus through a residency in a high school. The artists worked with A-level students on an interpretation of a Celtic story. The video includes observations from artists, teachers and students on planning, running and participating in a residency; and shows highlights from the residency which illustrate the value of artists-in-schools work.

If We Can Do That: Arts Residency Work at Mulberry School

Directed by Richard Coldman.

Available from:
Tower Hamlets Professional Development Centre
English Street
London E3 4TA.

This video documents the involvement of artists with a London secondary school for girls.

It shows the results of residencies from an international body of artists, working in a range of areas from circus skills to poetry; showing the role artists can play in helping schools to achieve high-quality arts work

Books about the arts in schools

The publications listed in this section give guidance on the arts in schools. They should be a useful starting point for artists wishing to learn more about the place of the arts in schools, and what is taught to pupils of different ages.

A Guide to the National Curriculum

School Curriculum and Assessment Authority (SCAA) and Awdurdod Cwricwlwm ac Asesu Cymru (ACAC) (1996).
ISBN: 1 85838 082 0.

Available from:
SCAA Publications   ACAC
PO Box 235   Castle Buildings
Hayes   Womanby Street
Middlesex UB3 1HF.   Cardiff CF1 9SX.

Briefing Paper 4: The Revised National Curriculum — the Changes to the Arts

Rick Rogers, Arts Council of England (1995).

Available from:
Education and Training Department
Arts Council of England.

The Arts in Schools: Principles, Practice and Provision

Ken Robinson, Calouste Gulbenkian Foundation (1989).
ISBN: 0 903319 23 3.

Available from:
Turnaround Distribution Ltd.

Setting the Scene: the Arts and Young People

Department of National Heritage (1996).

Available from:
DNH
2-4 Cockspur Street
London SW1Y 5DH.

Expressive Arts 5 – 14: Curriculum and Assessment in Scotland — National Guidelines

Scottish Office Education Department (1992).

Available from:
HMSO Scotland
71 Lothian Road
Edinburgh EH3 9AZ.

The Northern Ireland Curriculum. Key Stages 1 and 2: Programmes of Study and Attainment Targets

Department of Education for Northern Ireland (1996).
ISBN: 0 337 041590 X.

Available from:
HMSO Bookshop
16 Arthur Street
Belfast BT1 4CD.

The Northern Ireland Curriculum. Key Stages 3 and 4: Programmes of Study and Attainment Targets

Department of Education for Northern Ireland (1996).
ISBN: 0 337 04307 8.

Available from:
HMSO Bookshop, Belfast.

Art and design

Art in the National Curriculum

Department for Education and Welsh Office, HMSO (1995).
ISBN: 0 11 270890 0.

Available from:
HMSO Publications Centre
PO Box 276
London SW8 5DT.

Design and Technology in the National Curriculum

Department for Education and Welsh Office, HMSO (1995).
ISBN: 0 11 270888 9.

Available from:
HMSO Publications Centre.

Dance

Dance in Schools

Arts Council of England (1993).
ISBN: 0 7287 0655 5.

Available from:
Dance Department
Arts Council of England.

Physical Education in the National Curriculum

Department for Education and Welsh Office, HMSO (1995).
ISBN: 0 11 270892 7.

Available from:
HMSO Publications Centre.

English and Drama

English in the National Curriculum

Department for Education and Welsh Office, HMSO (1995).
ISBN: 0 11 270882 X.

Available from:
HMSO Publications Centre.

Drama in Schools

Arts Council of England (1992).
ISBN: 0 7287 0633 4.

Available from:
Drama Department
Arts Council of England.

Music

Music in the National Curriculum

Department for Education and Welsh Office, HMSO (1995).
ISBN: 0 11 270891 9.

Available from:
HMSO Publications Centre.

Photography

Creating Vision: Photography and the National Curriculum

Edited by Sue Isherwood and Nick Stanley, Arts Council of England (1994).
ISBN: 0 728706 68 7.

Available from:
Cornerhouse Publications
70 Oxford Street
Manchester M1 5NH.

Special educational needs

A Glossary of Special Education

Philip Williams, Open University Press (1988).
ISBN: 0 335 15995 8.

Available from:
Open University Educational Enterprises Ltd.
12 Cofferidge Close
Stony Stratford
Milton Keynes MK11 1BY.

David Fulton Publishers
have produced a series of books on
the curriculum for pupils with
special educational needs. The
ones listed below are concerned
with teaching the arts curriculum.

They are available from: David
Fulton Publishers Ltd.
2 Barbon Close
London WC1N 3JX.

**Art for All
I The Framework**

Melanie Peter, David Fulton
Publishers (1996).
ISBN: 1 85346 317 5.

**Art for All
II The Practice**

Melanie Peter, David Fulton
Publishers (1996).
ISBN: 1 85346 418 X.

Drama for All

Melanie Peter, David Fulton
Publishers (1994).
ISBN: 1 85346 315 9.

Music for All

Peter Wills and Melanie Peter,
David Fulton Publishers (1996).
ISBN: 1 85346 280 2.

Index